# Complaints to Cheers, Feedback to Gold:

## Mastering Complaints Management

Gerard Assey

# *Complaints to Cheers, Feedback to Gold: Mastering Complaints Management*

By

Gerard Assey



*Published by:*
Gerard Assey
19/18, Palli Arasan Street
Anna Nagar East
Chennai - 600 102

**ISBN:** 978-93-92492-80-8



*(Image by Freepik: 'https://www.freepik.com' Thank You)*

# Table of Contents

- ✓ Key Challenges Organizations Face when having to Deal with Complaints
- ✓ Steps and Strategies- Right from Receipt of Complaint to it Being Resolved and Afterwards
- ✓ Fostering a Complaint-Friendly Culture
- ✓ The Role of Leadership and Organizational Culture
- ✓ Sample Complaint Handling Scripts and Templates
- ✓ Case Studies of Successful Complaints Management
- ✓ Interesting and Engaging Training Games to Enhance Understanding
- ✓ Complaint Scenarios, Role-play Guides, and Evaluation Forms for use in the Training/ Games/Sessions
- ✓ Taking it Forward
- ✓ Conclusion
- ✓ About the Author

# Preface

Welcome to the world of Complaints Management, where customer feedback becomes a catalyst for growth and improvement. In today's competitive landscape, organizations that excel in understanding and addressing complaints stand out as true leaders in customer satisfaction and loyalty.

This book is a comprehensive guide that delves into the art and science of handling complaints, both from external customers and within an organization. It is designed to equip corporates and organizations with the knowledge and tools to proactively transform complaints into opportunities for enhancement.

At its core, Complaints Management is not just about conflict resolution but also about building a customer-centric culture that values feedback. We explore the psychology behind complaints, empowering readers to delve into the emotions and motivations driving customers and employees to voice their concerns.

Through the pages of this book, you will discover practical strategies for designing an effective complaints management process, nurturing active listening and empathy, conducting thorough investigations, and implementing preventive measures to avoid recurring issues. Additionally, we delve into the crucial role of leadership in fostering a complaint-friendly culture, where feedback is not only embraced but also integrated into the organization's values and mission.

From understanding different types of complaints to navigating difficult situations and crisis management, we leave no stone unturned in our pursuit of excellence in complaints management. Moreover, we emphasize the importance of data and analytics in identifying patterns, making informed decisions, and driving continuous improvement.

Our goal is to inspire readers to view complaints not as obstacles but as stepping stones to success. By implementing the strategies and techniques provided in this book, organizations can build stronger relationships with their customers, strengthen their reputation, and unlock new avenues for growth.

In closing, we encourage you to embark on this journey of Complaints Management, embracing the transformative power of feedback, and turning complaints into opportunities for improvement. As you read through these pages, we hope you find inspiration, practical guidance, and actionable insights that will propel your organization to new heights of success.

Thank you for choosing this book, and we wish you a rewarding and enlightening experience on your path to mastering Complaints Management.

# Setting the Stage for Effective Complaints Management

In the dynamic landscape of modern business, no organization is immune to complaints. They come in various forms - from customers unhappy with a product or service, to employees dissatisfied with their working conditions, to vendors raising concerns about payment delays. Complaints, in essence, are a natural byproduct of interactions in any organization.

In this introductory chapter, we'll delve into the significance of complaints management, exploring why it is a pivotal aspect of sustaining a thriving business. We'll also unravel the ramifications of ignoring or mishandling complaints, which extend far beyond a mere inconvenience. Finally, we'll set the goal of this book: to provide you, the reader, with the knowledge, strategies, and tools necessary to not only resolve complaints effectively but to also transform them into catalysts for improvement and growth.

## The Importance of Effective Complaints Management

Complaints are more than just grievances. They are powerful indicators of the health of your organization. When viewed through the right lens, complaints are like a compass guiding your path towards growth and success. Understanding their value is the first step in harnessing their potential.

The impact of unresolved complaints on businesses is multifaceted. When a complaint goes unaddressed or is poorly managed, it has the potential to tarnish your organization's reputation. In an era where customer reviews and social media can make or break a brand, a single unresolved complaint can reverberate across the internet, dissuading potential customers and affecting your bottom line.

Furthermore, unresolved complaints can erode customer loyalty. Customers who feel that their concerns are not taken seriously are more likely to take their business elsewhere. Loyal customers are the lifeblood of any business, and their loss can be costly.

Unaddressed employee complaints can wreak havoc on internal morale. Dissatisfied employees are less productive, more likely to leave their positions, and can even foster a negative workplace culture. In an era where hiring and retaining top talent is critical, this can be a significant detriment to your organization.

**Our Goal: Equip You for Effective Complaints Management**

The goal of this book is clear: we aim to equip you with the knowledge and tools to not only handle complaints efficiently but also to leverage them as opportunities for improvement. Complaints, when managed correctly, can be invaluable sources of feedback and insight. They can uncover systemic issues that, once addressed, can enhance product quality, customer service, and operational efficiency.

We believe that by the end of this book, you will not only be a proficient complaints handler but also a proactive seeker of improvement opportunities. You will have the expertise to turn disgruntled customers into loyal advocates, convert employee grievances into workplace enhancements, and ultimately bolster your organization's reputation and performance.

The journey begins here, with an understanding of the importance of effective complaints management. We invite you to explore the subsequent chapters, each designed to build your expertise in a structured manner.

By the end of this book, you will be equipped to not only manage complaints but to transform them into stepping stones on your path to organizational excellence.

# Why is this Subject so Important Today? The Benefits!

The subject of complaints management is more critical today than ever for organizations due to several factors, including heightened customer expectations, increased competition, and the rise of social media. Properly resolving complaints on time has become a crucial aspect of maintaining a positive brand reputation and building customer loyalty. Here are the benefits to employees, the organization, and stakeholders in effectively handling complaints:

**Benefits to Employees:**

- ✓ Job Satisfaction and Morale: Resolving complaints efficiently leads to positive customer feedback, recognition, and a sense of accomplishment for employees, contributing to higher job satisfaction and morale.
- ✓ Reduced Stress and Burnout: Promptly addressing complaints prevents them from escalating and reduces stress for employees who would otherwise have to deal with prolonged and complex issues.
- ✓ Skill Development: Handling complaints provides employees with opportunities to develop essential skills, such as communication, empathy, problem-solving, and conflict resolution.
- ✓ Example: A customer service representative successfully resolves a complex complaint, receiving appreciation from the customer and boosting their confidence in handling challenging situations.

**Benefits to the Organization:**

- ✓ Customer Loyalty and Retention: Properly resolving complaints builds trust and loyalty among customers, leading to increased customer retention and repeat business.
- ✓ Enhanced Reputation: Organizations known for their excellent complaint resolution gain a positive reputation, attracting more customers and differentiating themselves from competitors.
- ✓ Competitive Advantage: Effective complaint management can be a powerful competitive advantage, as customers are more likely to choose a company with a reputation for exceptional customer service.
- ✓ Example: An e-commerce company's efficient complaint handling process leads to positive reviews and word-of-mouth referrals, setting them apart from competitors with similar products.

**Benefits to Stakeholders:**

- ✓ Increased Customer Satisfaction: Properly resolved complaints result in higher customer satisfaction, leading to increased customer loyalty and positive recommendations.
- ✓ Stronger Relationships: Addressing complaints demonstrates an organization's commitment to meeting customer needs, fostering strong relationships with customers and stakeholders.
- ✓ Positive Brand Perception: Organizations with a reputation for excellent complaint resolution enjoy a positive brand perception, attracting investors and strategic partnerships.

- ✓ Example: A hotel chain's proactive complaint resolution approach results in satisfied customers who share their positive experiences on social media, generating more business and investor interest.
- ✓ Crisis Prevention: Properly resolving complaints in a timely manner prevents issues from escalating into full-blown crises that could damage the organization's reputation.
- ✓ Example: A retail company responds swiftly and effectively to customer complaints about a product recall, minimizing negative media coverage and maintaining customer trust.

As seen, effective complaints management is critical for organizations to stay competitive, retain customers, and maintain a positive brand image. By valuing customer feedback, resolving complaints promptly and professionally, and continuously improving processes, organizations can foster a culture of customer-centricity and long-term success. Investing in complaint resolution yields significant benefits for employees, the organization, and stakeholders, creating a virtuous cycle of customer satisfaction and growth.

# The Impact, Repercussions and Consequences of Unresolved Complaints

The impact of not resolving complaints or not doing so properly and on time can have severe repercussions for organizations. It can significantly affect their credibility, image, reputation, customer loyalty, and overall business success. Here are some of the consequences:

- ✓ Damaged Credibility: Failing to address complaints promptly and adequately undermines an organization's credibility and trustworthiness. Customers may perceive the organization as indifferent or uncaring, leading to a loss of faith in its ability to deliver on promises.
- ✓ Negative Word-of-Mouth: Unsatisfied customers are more likely to share their negative experiences with others. This negative word-of-mouth can spread quickly through social media, review platforms, and word-of-mouth referrals, damaging the organization's reputation.
- ✓ Customer Churn: Unresolved or poorly handled complaints can result in customer churn, as dissatisfied customers may switch to competitors who provide better service and complaint resolution.
- ✓ Decreased Customer Loyalty: When complaints are ignored or not adequately resolved, customers may feel unvalued and

become less loyal to the organization, seeking alternatives with better customer service.

- ✓ Brand Damage: A pattern of unresolved complaints can tarnish an organization's brand image and create a negative perception in the market. This can lead to decreased customer interest and decreased revenue.
- ✓ Legal and Regulatory Issues: Ignoring certain types of complaints, such as those related to legal or regulatory matters, can lead to potential legal consequences and damage the organization's reputation in the eyes of stakeholders.
- ✓ Employee Dissatisfaction: Employees who witness ineffective complaint resolution may become disheartened and lose confidence in the organization's commitment to customer satisfaction. This can impact employee morale and productivity.
- ✓ Loss of Business Opportunities: A negative reputation resulting from mishandled complaints can deter potential customers and business partners from engaging with the organization.
- ✓ Crisis Escalation: Neglecting complaints can lead to unresolved issues accumulating and escalating into full-blown crises that require significant resources and crisis management efforts.
- ✓ Missed Improvement Opportunities: Failing to address complaints means missing valuable opportunities for improvement and innovation. Customer feedback can provide insights into areas that need enhancement, leading to lost

chances to optimize products, services, and processes.

- ✓ Example: A restaurant consistently receives complaints about slow service, but the management ignores them, assuming the complaints are isolated incidents. Over time, negative reviews and feedback on social media accumulate, leading to a decline in foot traffic and a damaged reputation.

In contrast, an organization that proactively and effectively addresses complaints can benefit from increased customer loyalty, positive word-of-mouth, and a strengthened reputation. By acknowledging and resolving complaints in a timely and empathetic manner, organizations demonstrate their commitment to customer satisfaction and showcase their dedication to continuous improvement. Properly resolved complaints can turn dissatisfied customers into loyal advocates, contributing to sustainable business growth and success.

# Key Skills, Attributes and Traits to Effectively Handle Complaints

To be highly effective and successful in handling complaints, individuals need to possess a combination of key skills, attributes, and traits that enable them to navigate emotional situations, communicate effectively, and provide satisfactory resolutions. Here are some essential qualities:

- ✓ Empathy and Active Listening:
  Skill: The ability to put oneself in the complainant's shoes and genuinely understand their perspective.
  Example: A customer service representative listens attentively to a frustrated customer, showing understanding and empathy for their concerns, even if the issue was not directly caused by the company.
- ✓ Communication Skills:
  Skill: Clear and effective communication, both in written and verbal form, to ensure the complainant's concerns are understood and addressed.
  Example: A complaint handler communicates the steps being taken to resolve the complaint, provides regular updates, and ensures the complainant is informed throughout the process.
- ✓ Problem-Solving Skills:
  Skill: The capability to analyze complex complaints, identify root causes, and devise practical solutions.
  Example: An IT support specialist investigates a recurring software issue based on user

complaints, identifies a programming bug, and coordinates with the development team to implement a fix.

- ✓ Patience and Resilience:
  Attribute: The ability to remain calm and composed when dealing with difficult or emotional complainants.
  Example: A customer service representative handles a barrage of complaints during a busy period with patience and maintains a positive attitude in finding solutions.
- ✓ Conflict Resolution:
  Skill: The capacity to mediate and find common ground between parties with conflicting interests.
  Example: A team leader resolves a workplace conflict by listening to both parties, identifying common goals, and facilitating compromise.
- ✓ Time Management:
  Skill: Efficiently prioritizing and managing multiple complaints to ensure timely responses and resolutions.
  Example: A complaint handler prioritizes urgent complaints over routine inquiries, ensuring that no issues fall through the cracks.
- ✓ Cultural Sensitivity:
  Attribute: The awareness and respect for diverse backgrounds, ensuring complaints from various cultural perspectives are handled with cultural sensitivity.
  Example: A global customer support team ensures that complaints from customers in different countries are handled with consideration for cultural nuances and preferences.

- ✓ Accountability:
  Trait: Taking responsibility for resolving complaints and ensuring that commitments made are upheld.
  Example: A manager takes ownership of a customer complaint, personally following up on its resolution, and offering compensation as a gesture of goodwill.
- ✓ Analytical Thinking:
  Skill: The ability to analyze data from complaints, identifying patterns and trends to address systemic issues.
  Example: A product manager uses complaints data to identify a recurring defect and proposes product improvements to prevent further complaints.
- ✓ Flexibility and Adaptability:
  Attribute: The capacity to adapt strategies and approaches to suit individual complainants and unique situations.
  Example: A human resources professional tailors their approach to resolving an employee complaint based on the complainant's preferred communication style and needs.
- ✓ Conflict Resolution:
  Skill: Ability to mediate and find common ground between parties with conflicting interests.
  Example: A team leader resolves a workplace conflict by listening to both parties, identifying common goals, and facilitating compromise.

By cultivating these skills, attributes, and traits, individuals can not only effectively handle complaints but also turn them into opportunities for positive outcomes, contributing to overall customer satisfaction and organizational success.

# Understanding Complaints

Complaints are the voice of those who interact with your organization - customers, employees, vendors, and more. They are not mere grievances; they are vital feedback mechanisms that can shape the present and future of your business. In this chapter, we will delve into the intricate world of complaints, exploring their definition, differentiation from feedback and criticisms, the psychology that drives them, their significance as fountains of information, and their inextricable link to business performance.

**Defining Complaints: Beyond Grievances**

A complaint is not a synonym for criticism or feedback, although they share some common elements. Complaints are, by nature, expressions of discontent, dissatisfaction, or displeasure. They are usually directed towards a particular individual, department, or the organization as a whole, signaling a perceived failure to meet expectations or standards. The differentiation between a complaint, feedback, and criticism often lies in the emotional intensity behind the message and the expectation of resolution. Complaints are typically laden with a sense of urgency and a desire for resolution.

**The Psychology of Complaints: Why People Complain**

Understanding the psychology behind complaints is paramount to effective management. People complain for a myriad of reasons, and it often goes beyond the immediate issue at hand. Complaints are emotional expressions driven by various underlying factors, such as:

- ✓ **Unfulfilled Expectations:** When customers or employees have expectations that are not met, they may complain. These expectations can be based on past experiences, advertisements, promises, or industry norms.
- ✓ **Frustration:** Customers can become frustrated when a product or service fails to function as expected or when they face difficulties in their interactions with your organization. This frustration is a common trigger for complaints.
- ✓ **Injustice:** If people feel they have been treated unfairly, they are more likely to complain. This can include perceptions of discrimination, unequal treatment, or unethical behavior.
- ✓ **Voice as Power:** For some, complaining is a way to assert their voice and demand attention. It's a means of making their concerns known and, hopefully, effecting change.

**The Significance of Customer and Employee Complaints**

Complaints are not nuisances to be minimized; they are valuable sources of information. Both customer and employee complaints provide unique insights that can significantly impact your organization. They serve as the proverbial canaries in the coal mine, warning of underlying issues that, if left unaddressed, can have more profound consequences.

For customers, complaints can highlight flaws in your products, services, or processes. When managed effectively, they offer an opportunity to recover customer trust and, in some cases, even turn dissatisfied customers into loyal advocates. Every complaint can be seen as a chance to improve your offerings and enhance the overall customer experience.

In the realm of employee complaints, they often indicate deeper issues that can harm morale and productivity. Addressing these complaints not only improves employee satisfaction but can also lead to a more positive workplace culture. Engaged and satisfied employees are more likely to contribute to your organization's success.

**The Link Between Complaints and Business Performance**

Complaints are not isolated incidents; they are interconnected with the broader performance of your organization. When managed effectively, they can be catalysts for improvement. Here's how:

- ✓ **Product and Service Improvement:** Customer complaints can uncover flaws in your products or services. Addressing these issues leads to product enhancements, increased customer satisfaction, and, ultimately, higher sales.
- ✓ **Operational Efficiency:** Employee complaints about internal processes can reveal bottlenecks and inefficiencies. By addressing these concerns, you can streamline operations, improve productivity, and reduce costs.
- ✓ **Reputation Management:** Handling complaints with empathy and efficiency enhances your reputation. Satisfied customers and employees become advocates, which can attract more business and top talent.

**Action Plan:**

- ✓ **Differentiation Workshop:** Conduct a workshop with your team to differentiate between complaints, feedback, and criticisms. Use real-life examples to illustrate these differences.
- ✓ **Psychology Insights:** Study the psychology of complaints to understand the emotional undercurrents. Discuss common triggers for complaints and ways to address them effectively.
- ✓ **Complaint Analysis:** Start analyzing past complaints to identify recurring themes and root causes. This will be a foundation for future improvements.
- ✓ **Link to Business Goals:** Link your complaints management to broader business goals. Discuss how effective complaint management can improve product quality, customer satisfaction, and overall performance.

**Example:**

Consider a scenario where a customer complains about a software bug that resulted in data loss. At first glance, this seems like a technical issue. However, delving deeper, you realize that the customer's emotional reaction is driven by the fear of losing critical business data. Understanding this psychological aspect can guide the complaint resolution process, which goes beyond fixing the bug to reassuring the customer about data recovery and implementing additional data protection measures.

In this chapter, we've laid the foundation for understanding the intricate world of complaints. Complaints are not just problems to be solved; they are opportunities to enhance your organization and build stronger relationships with customers and employees.

As you continue through this book, you'll gain the tools and knowledge to manage complaints effectively, turning them into catalysts for positive change.

# Types of Complaints

Complaints are not a one-size-fits-all phenomenon; they come in various forms and from different sources. In this chapter, we'll explore the intricacies of categorizing complaints, the nuances of complaints from customers and employees, and the differentiation between product/service-related and process-related complaints. We'll also discuss the significance of recognizing patterns and trends in these complaints and the vital distinction between isolated incidents and systemic issues.

**Categorizing Complaints:**

*(Internal vs. External, Customer vs. Employee, Product/Service vs. Process)*

Complaints can be categorized in several ways, offering a comprehensive view of the issues that affect an organization:

- ✓ Internal vs. External Complaints:

  *Internal Complaints:* These originate from within the organization and are typically raised by employees. They may pertain to workplace conditions, HR matters, or process inefficiencies.

  *External Complaints:* These come from external sources, primarily customers. They concern products, services, billing, and interactions with the organization.

- ✓ Customer vs. Employee Complaints:

  *Customer Complaints:* These are grievances expressed by customers regarding their experiences with your organization, including dissatisfaction with products, services, or interactions.

*Employee Complaints:* These complaints are raised by employees about issues such as workplace conditions, management practices, or interpersonal conflicts.

- ✓ Product/Service vs. Process-Related Complaints:

  *Product/Service-Related Complaints:* These complaints revolve around the quality, functionality, or delivery of products or services. Common examples include defective products, late deliveries, or unsatisfactory services.

  *Process-Related Complaints:* These are focused on the internal processes of the organization. They may involve bottlenecks, inefficiencies, or complicated procedures that affect both customers and employees.

**Analyzing Patterns and Trends in Complaints**

To effectively manage complaints, it's essential to analyze patterns and trends within different complaint categories. Recognizing recurrent issues and common threads can guide your organization in making informed decisions for improvement. Here's how to do it:

- ✓ Data Collection: Gather complaint data systematically. Implement a digital system to record and categorize complaints. This enables you to access data quickly and analyze it effectively.
- ✓ Data Analysis: Regularly review the data to identify patterns. Pay attention to recurring issues, specific products or services involved, and the departments or processes linked to the complaints.

- ✓ Root Cause Analysis: Dive deep into patterns to uncover the root causes. Are complaints related to a specific supplier, a particular process step, or a specific location? Identifying root causes is vital for effective resolution.
- ✓ Trend Analysis: Extend your analysis to observe long-term trends. Are complaints increasing or decreasing? How does this relate to actions taken to address them?

**The Importance of Distinguishing Between Individual Incidents and Systemic Issues**

Not all complaints are created equal. Some are isolated incidents, while others point to systemic issues. Distinguishing between the two is crucial for effective resolution:

- ✓ Individual Incidents: These are one-off complaints arising from specific, isolated incidents. They often result from unusual circumstances and require individualized resolutions. For instance, a customer receiving a damaged product due to mishandling during shipping is an individual incident.
- ✓ Systemic Issues: These are recurrent complaints stemming from underlying problems within the organization. These issues impact multiple customers or employees and require systemic changes to address. For example, multiple customers complaining about slow delivery times may indicate a systemic issue with the supply chain.

**Action Plan:**

- ✓ Categorization Workshop: Conduct a workshop to help your team understand the different categories of complaints and how to categorize them effectively.
- ✓ Data Analysis Training: Provide training on data collection and analysis methods. Encourage team members to look for patterns and trends in the complaint data.
- ✓ Root Cause Analysis: Train your team in root cause analysis techniques. Equip them to dig deeper into complaints to identify and address the underlying issues.
- ✓ Trend Monitoring: Implement a system to continuously monitor and report on complaint trends. Set up regular reviews to discuss long-term trends and take appropriate actions.

**Example:**

Imagine you run a retail business, and you've been receiving several complaints from customers about incorrect product deliveries. After analyzing the data, you realize there are two categories of complaints:

- ✓ Individual Incidents: Some complaints were due to genuine mix-ups in the order. These can be resolved by ensuring correct packaging and labeling during the shipping process.
- ✓ Systemic Issues: However, a significant number of complaints indicated a systemic issue in your order processing system. The root cause analysis reveals that your inventory management software wasn't syncing correctly, leading to order inaccuracies. Resolving these systemic issues is essential to prevent future complaints of this nature.

As noted, this chapter emphasizes the importance of categorizing complaints, recognizing patterns and trends, and distinguishing between individual incidents and systemic issues. This understanding is pivotal for your organization's efforts in improving products, services, and internal processes, ultimately enhancing customer and employee satisfaction.

# The Complaints Management Process

We'll now embark on a journey through the establishment of an effective complaints management process. This process is the cornerstone of successful complaint resolution, ensuring that grievances are not only addressed but also used as stepping stones for organizational improvement. We will explore each step in detail, from designing user-friendly complaint submission channels to assigning responsibilities, and setting clear timelines for response and resolution.

**Step-by-Step Guide to Establishing an Effective Complaints Management Process**

1. Identification and Receipt of Complaints:
   Begin by creating clear and accessible channels for complaints to be submitted. This can include a dedicated email address, a web form, a helpline, or even in-person options for customers and employees. The key is to make it as easy as possible for individuals to express their grievances.
2. Recording and Categorization:
   Once a complaint is received, it should be documented systematically. Include information about the complainant, the nature of the complaint, and its source. Categorize complaints based on their type (customer or employee, product-related or process-related, etc.).
3. Acknowledgment and Triage:
   Acknowledge the receipt of the complaint promptly. This acknowledgment assures the

complainant that their concerns are being taken seriously. Assess the severity of the complaint and prioritize it accordingly.

4. Investigation and Root Cause Analysis:
   Dive deep into the complaint to identify the root cause. This often involves consulting relevant departments, gathering information, and speaking with the complainant if necessary.
5. Resolution Planning:
   Develop a clear plan for resolution. This might involve coordinating with other departments, creating an action plan, and setting milestones for resolution.
6. Resolution Execution:
   Put the resolution plan into action. Ensure that all responsible parties are aware of their roles and that the process is progressing as planned.
7. Communication:
   Keep the complainant informed throughout the process. Regular updates and clear communication are essential. Even if the resolution takes time, transparency is key.
8. Verification and Validation:
   Once the resolution is executed, verify that it meets the complainant's expectations. In some cases, it might be necessary to seek their validation to ensure their satisfaction.
9. Closing and Documentation:
   Close the complaint officially and document the entire process. This documentation is not just for record-keeping; it's valuable for identifying trends and preventing similar issues in the future.

10. Feedback Loop:
    Ensure that lessons learned from each complaint are integrated into your processes. Feedback should be a cyclical process, driving continuous improvement.

**Designing User-Friendly Complaint Submission Channels**

**Example:** Consider a multinational e-commerce company. They offer multiple complaint submission channels, including a web form, email, a 24/7 helpline, and in-person complaint desks at their major warehouses. These options cater to the diverse preferences of their customers. The web form is user-friendly, with clear fields and easy navigation. The helpline is staffed with knowledgeable agents who can guide customers through the complaint submission process. Each channel is designed to make it as convenient as possible for customers to express their concerns.

**Assigning Responsibility: The Role of Frontline Staff, Supervisors, and Dedicated Complaint Handlers**

- ✓ Frontline Staff: These are often the first point of contact for complaints. They should be trained to acknowledge complaints, record initial information, and escalate them to the appropriate department or complaint handlers.
- ✓ Supervisors: Supervisors play a crucial role in triaging complaints, ensuring they are assigned to the right teams, and monitoring the resolution process. They provide the bridge between frontline staff and dedicated complaint handlers.
- ✓ Dedicated Complaint Handlers: These individuals have the expertise to investigate

and resolve complaints effectively. They might work closely with other departments, such as quality control or HR, to address systemic issues.

**Setting Clear Timelines for Response and Resolution**

Timeliness is paramount in complaints management. When complainants see prompt actions, it reinforces their trust in your organization. Clear timelines should be set for both response and resolution:

- ✓ Response Time: Aim to acknowledge complaints within a specific timeframe, often within 24-48 hours. Even if resolution takes longer, this initial response is crucial for complainant reassurance.
- ✓ Resolution Time: Depending on the complexity of the complaint, set reasonable but specific timelines for resolution. These may vary from a few days to several weeks, but clarity is key.

**Action Plan:**

- ✓ Channel Audit: Conduct an audit of your current complaint submission channels. Assess their user-friendliness and consider adding or improving channels where needed.
- ✓ Responsibility Mapping: Clearly define the roles and responsibilities of frontline staff, supervisors, and dedicated complaint handlers. Ensure they are trained adequately.
- ✓ Timelines and Service Level Agreements (SLAs): Develop SLAs for complaint response and resolution. Make sure they are realistic and achievable.
- ✓ Feedback Integration: Create mechanisms to integrate feedback from complaints into your

organizational processes, ensuring that they drive positive change.

**Example:**

A renowned restaurant chain recognized the need to streamline their complaints management process. They implemented a user-friendly mobile app for customers to submit complaints, which streamlined the process. The frontline staff at each restaurant were trained to acknowledge complaints and escalate them to a centralized team responsible for resolution. Timelines were set for acknowledgment (within 24 hours) and resolution (within 7 days for standard complaints). A feedback loop was established to share insights from complaints with their chefs and kitchen staff to continually improve the dining experience.

We've effectively covered the intricacies of establishing an effective complaints management process. This process is the backbone of transforming complaints into opportunities for growth. It ensures that grievances are addressed promptly, and the organization benefits from each interaction, ultimately leading to a more robust, customer-centric, and efficient operation.

# Active Listening and Empathy

In the realm of complaints management, active listening and empathy are not just skills; they are essential tools for building rapport and resolving issues effectively. This chapter delves into the art of active listening, the role of empathy, and the importance of training employees in these critical aspects of complaints management.

**The Art of Active Listening: Techniques for Genuinely Understanding Complainants' Perspectives**

Active listening is the foundation of effective complaints management. It goes beyond merely hearing words; it involves fully comprehending the complainant's perspective. Here are techniques to master the art of active listening:

- ✓ **Give Undivided Attention:** When a complainant speaks, give them your complete attention. This means maintaining eye contact, nodding occasionally, and avoiding interruptions.
- ✓ **Paraphrase and Clarify:** After the complainant has expressed their concern, paraphrase it in your words to ensure you understand correctly. This not only shows that you're actively listening but also gives the complainant an opportunity to clarify their point.
- ✓ **Ask Open-Ended Questions:** Encourage the complainant to provide more information by asking open-ended questions. These questions cannot be answered with a simple

"yes" or "no" and can help uncover deeper issues.

- ✓ **Reflect Feelings:** Recognize and validate the complainant's emotions. For example, you might say, "I can understand why you're frustrated about this," which demonstrates empathy and understanding.
- ✓ **Avoid Making Assumptions:** Do not assume you know the entire situation. Let the complainant express themselves fully before drawing conclusions.

**The Role of Empathy in Complaints Management: Showing Empathy Without Admitting Fault**

Empathy is the ability to understand and share the feelings of another without necessarily admitting fault. It's a powerful tool for building trust and rapport with complainants. Here's how to show empathy without admitting fault:

- ✓ **Acknowledge Emotions:** Recognize the complainant's emotions and express understanding. For instance, "I understand this situation has been frustrating for you."
- ✓ **Apologize for the Experience:** Apologize for the inconvenience or negative experience without necessarily admitting wrongdoing. For example, "I'm sorry you've had this experience."
- ✓ **Promise Action:** Ensure the complainant that their concern will be addressed. Make it clear that you are taking their complaint seriously.
- ✓ **Avoid Blame:** While showing empathy, refrain from blaming or admitting fault prematurely. Stick to the facts and avoid making judgments.

**Training Employees in Active Listening and Empathy**

Active listening and empathy can be learned and refined. Here's how to train employees in these critical skills:

- ✓ **Workshops and Role-Playing:** Conduct workshops that teach active listening techniques and empathy. Use role-playing scenarios to help employees practice these skills.
- ✓ **Mentoring and Shadowing:** Pair new employees with experienced ones to observe and learn effective complaint handling. Encourage them to ask questions and seek guidance.
- ✓ **Feedback and Coaching:** Provide regular feedback and coaching. Review recorded interactions with complainants to identify areas for improvement and commend excellent practices.
- ✓ **Continuous Learning:** Encourage employees to engage in continuous learning. Share resources, articles, and books on active listening and empathy in complaints management.

**Example:**

Imagine a customer contacts a telecom company with a complaint about a billing error. The customer service representative actively listens by allowing the customer to explain the issue fully. The representative paraphrases the customer's concern, asking, "So, if I understand correctly, you received a bill that was much higher than you expected, and it doesn't match your usage." This demonstrates active listening.

In showing empathy, the representative acknowledges the customer's frustration and promises to resolve the issue promptly. They say, "I can understand how frustrating this must be for you. I'm truly sorry for the inconvenience you've experienced. We'll investigate this immediately and make sure it's corrected."

This example illustrates how active listening and empathy can be applied in a real complaint handling scenario, ultimately leading to a more satisfied customer.

In this chapter, we've explored the art of active listening and the role of empathy in complaints management. These skills are vital for building trust, understanding the complainant's perspective, and ultimately resolving complaints effectively. By training your employees in active listening and empathy, you equip them with the tools to transform disgruntled customers into loyal advocates.

# Investigating Complaints

Effective complaints management goes beyond listening and empathy; it involves thorough investigation. This chapter explores the process of gathering relevant information and evidence for a comprehensive investigation. It also addresses the nuances of dealing with emotional or difficult complainants and the importance of involving relevant stakeholders in the investigation process.

**Gathering Relevant Information and Evidence for a Thorough Investigation**

- ✓ **Information Collection:** Begin by gathering as much information as possible from the complainant. This might include details of the incident, dates, times, locations, people involved, and any relevant documentation.
- ✓ **Documentation Review:** Examine relevant records, documents, and policies that may shed light on the complaint. This might include invoices, contracts, communication records, or standard operating procedures.
- ✓ **Witness Interviews:** If applicable, speak with witnesses who can provide additional insights. Their perspectives can corroborate or clarify details of the complaint.
- ✓ **Data Analysis:** In cases involving process-related complaints, data analysis may be necessary. For example, if the complaint is about slow service, analyzing service times over a period can provide valuable insights.
- ✓ **Expert Opinions:** In some cases, it may be necessary to seek expert opinions or

consultations, particularly in complex technical complaints.

**Establishing a Chain of Evidence:** Maintain a chain of evidence to ensure the integrity of collected data. This is vital if the complaint may result in legal or regulatory action.

**Dealing with Emotional or Difficult Complainants**

- ✓ **Emotion Acknowledgment:** When dealing with emotional complainants, acknowledge their emotions without judgment. For instance, "I understand that you're very upset about this situation."
- ✓ **Patient Listening:** Allow emotional complainants to express themselves fully. Sometimes, simply venting can help alleviate their frustration.
- ✓ **Empathy:** Show empathy and understanding without admitting fault. It's about recognizing their emotions, not necessarily agreeing with their perspective.
- ✓ **Stay Calm:** Maintain a calm and professional demeanor. Emotional complainants may escalate situations, and your composure can help diffuse tensions.
- ✓ **Set Boundaries:** While allowing them to express themselves, establish boundaries for respectful communication. Ensure the conversation remains constructive.

**Involving Relevant Stakeholders in the Investigation Process**

- ✓ **Interdepartmental Collaboration:** In cases where the complaint pertains to multiple departments or aspects of the organization, involve representatives from these areas in the investigation. Collaboration ensures a holistic view of the situation.

- ✓ **Legal and Compliance Teams:** When legal or compliance implications are involved, seek guidance from legal and compliance experts. They can advise on the proper course of action and ensure regulatory compliance.
- ✓ **Communication with Complainants:** Keep complainants informed about the involvement of relevant stakeholders in the investigation process. Transparency builds trust.

**Action Plan:**

- ✓ **Investigation Checklists:** Develop checklists to guide employees through the investigation process, ensuring they don't miss critical steps.
- ✓ **Emotional Intelligence Training:** Provide training in emotional intelligence for employees involved in complaints management. This equips them to handle emotional or difficult complainants effectively.
- ✓ **Collaboration Protocols:** Establish clear protocols for interdepartmental collaboration in the investigation process. Define roles, responsibilities, and communication channels.

**Example:**

Suppose a manufacturing company receives a complaint from a customer who experienced a product malfunction, leading to significant damage in their facility. The investigation process involves:

- ✓ **Information Collection:** The customer provides photos, videos, and detailed descriptions of the incident. The company reviews the product specifications and manufacturing records.

- ✓ **Witness Interviews:** Interviews are conducted with the customer's maintenance personnel who witnessed the incident, offering valuable insights.
- ✓ **Data Analysis:** The company reviews data logs from the product's sensors to understand the events leading to the malfunction.
- ✓ **Expert Opinion:** An independent engineering expert is consulted to evaluate the product's design and performance.
- ✓ **Legal Team Involvement:** The company's legal team is involved to assess potential liability and regulatory requirements.

Throughout this process, the complainant is kept informed about the progress and the involvement of relevant stakeholders, ensuring transparency in the investigation.

We've, in this chapter, effectively explored the vital aspects of investigating complaints. A comprehensive investigation is the key to resolving issues effectively, preventing future recurrences, and maintaining trust with complainants. By training employees to gather evidence, handle emotional complainants, and collaborate with relevant stakeholders, you empower your team to navigate the intricacies of complaints management successfully.

# Root Cause Analysis

Root cause analysis is the cornerstone of complaints management. It delves into the core of complaints, aiming to identify and address underlying issues rather than merely treating symptoms. This chapter explores how to identify root causes, the tools and methodologies for conducting effective root cause analysis, and preventative measures to avoid recurring complaints.

**Identifying Root Causes Behind Complaints to Address Underlying Issues**

- ✓ **Defining the Problem:** Begin by defining the problem clearly. What is the complaint, and what specific issue does it point to? A precise problem statement is essential.
- ✓ **The "Five Whys":** One of the simplest yet effective tools for root cause analysis is the "Five Whys" technique. It involves asking "why" repeatedly to drill down to the root cause. For example, if the complaint is about a delayed product delivery, asking "why" might lead to factors like inefficient logistics or supply chain issues.
- ✓ **Fishbone Diagram (Ishikawa):** Use a fishbone diagram to visually represent potential causes of the issue. Categories like people, process, equipment, and environment can help structure the analysis.
- ✓ **Brainstorming:** Involve a diverse team in brainstorming sessions to explore potential causes and contributing factors.
- ✓ **Data Analysis:** If data is available, quantitative analysis can reveal patterns and

trends that lead to root causes. This might involve statistical techniques or data mining.

**Tools and Methodologies for Conducting Effective Root Cause Analysis**

- ✓ **Pareto Analysis:** The Pareto principle, often known as the 80/20 rule, posits that roughly 80% of effects come from 20% of causes. Identifying and focusing on the significant causes can be a highly effective strategy.
- ✓ **Failure Mode and Effects Analysis (FMEA):** FMEA is a systematic, proactive method for evaluating potential failure modes within a process or product and their effects.
- ✓ **SWOT Analysis:** A SWOT analysis can help identify internal strengths and weaknesses (potential root causes) that may contribute to complaints.
- ✓ **PDCA (Plan-Do-Check-Act):** This iterative four-step management method can be used to improve processes continuously. It involves identifying problems, planning solutions, implementing changes, and reviewing results.
- ✓ **Root Cause Analysis Software:** Utilize specialized software tools that help organize data, visualize causes, and track progress.

**Preventative Measures: How to Avoid Recurring Complaints**

- ✓ **Action Plans:** Develop specific action plans to address root causes. These plans should detail what actions will be taken, who is responsible, and the timeline for completion.
- ✓ **Training and Education:** Provide necessary training to employees to prevent issues related to root causes. For instance, if a product quality issue is a root cause,

employees involved in quality control may need additional training.

- ✓ **Process Improvement:** Continuously improve processes to address root causes. For example, if a root cause is frequent miscommunication, implement a new communication protocol.
- ✓ **Monitoring and Feedback:** Implement systems to monitor processes and collect feedback from both employees and customers. This helps identify early signs of recurring issues.

**Action Plan:**

- ✓ **Root Cause Training:** Provide comprehensive training in root cause analysis techniques and methodologies to employees involved in complaints management.
- ✓ **Root Cause Action Plans:** Develop standardized action plan templates for addressing root causes. These templates should be used for each root cause identified.
- ✓ **Continuous Improvement Culture:** Foster a culture of continuous improvement within the organization. Encourage employees to proactively identify and address potential root causes.

**Example:**

A hospital receives a complaint regarding a medication error that led to patient harm. Root cause analysis is conducted:

- ✓ **The Problem:** Medication errors leading to patient harm.
- ✓ **Five Whys:** Asking "why" multiple times reveals that the root cause was lack of a

standardized medication administration process.

- ✓ **Fishbone Diagram:** A fishbone diagram illustrates contributing factors like lack of training, communication breakdown, and insufficient double-check processes.
- ✓ **Preventative Measures:** The hospital develops a comprehensive action plan that includes standardized medication administration protocols, additional training for staff, and improved communication during handovers. The plan is implemented, and medication error incidents decrease significantly.

As seen, root cause analysis as a fundamental process in complaints management. By using various tools and methodologies, organizations can identify and address the root causes of complaints, ultimately preventing their recurrence and improving overall operational efficiency.

# Resolving Complaints

Resolving complaints effectively is not only about addressing immediate issues but also about rebuilding trust and turning complainants into satisfied customers. In this chapter, we'll explore the development of effective resolution strategies, offering appropriate remedies and compensation, and leveraging complaints as opportunities for service recovery.

**Developing Effective Resolution Strategies**

- ✓ **Individualized Solutions:** Recognize that each complaint is unique. Tailor solutions to fit the specific circumstances of the complaint. For example, if a customer receives a damaged product, offer a replacement or a refund based on their preference.
- ✓ **Promptness:** Timeliness is crucial. Ensure that resolution efforts are initiated as soon as possible after the complaint is received. Delay can exacerbate complainants' frustration.
- ✓ **Communication:** Maintain open and transparent communication with the complainant throughout the resolution process. Keep them updated on the progress and any expected delays.
- ✓ **Empowerment of Frontline Staff:** Equip frontline employees with the authority and resources to resolve complaints at their level whenever possible. This can expedite solutions and minimize escalation.
- ✓ **Escalation Protocols:** In cases where complaints cannot be resolved at the frontline, establish clear protocols for escalation. Define

the criteria for escalation and the roles of supervisors or dedicated complaint handlers.

**Offering Appropriate Remedies and Compensation**

- ✓ **Apologies:** A sincere apology can go a long way in resolving complaints. It acknowledges the inconvenience or dissatisfaction experienced by the complainant.
- ✓ **Refunds and Replacements:** Offer refunds, replacements, or exchanges for products or services that did not meet the complainant's expectations.
- ✓ **Discounts or Coupons:** In certain cases, offering discounts on future purchases or coupons can be a way to compensate for the inconvenience caused.
- ✓ **Service Recovery:** Beyond compensatory measures, service recovery involves going the extra mile to ensure the complainant leaves with a positive perception. For instance, offering a complimentary service or a hand-written note of apology.
- ✓ **Policy Reevaluation:** If a complaint reveals an issue with existing policies or procedures, be willing to revisit and revise these to prevent future occurrences.

**Turning Complaints into Opportunities for Service Recovery**

- ✓ **Surveys and Feedback:** Encourage complainants to provide feedback on the resolution process. Their insights can help identify areas for improvement.
- ✓ **Continuous Improvement:** Use the data and insights from complaints to enhance

processes, train employees, and prevent similar issues from recurring.

- ✓ **Customer Engagement:** Engage with the complainant post-resolution to ensure their satisfaction and willingness to continue doing business with your organization.

**Action Plan:**

- ✓ **Resolution Strategy Templates:** Develop templates for resolution strategies that employees can use. These templates should include guidelines for assessing each complaint and determining appropriate remedies.
- ✓ **Communication Training:** Provide training in effective communication for employees involved in complaints management. Ensure they can convey apologies and updates professionally and empathetically.
- ✓ **Feedback Loops:** Establish feedback loops within the organization, ensuring that insights from complaints drive improvements. Regularly review resolution data and take action to prevent recurring issues.

**Example:**

A hotel guest complains about a subpar experience during their stay, including a malfunctioning air conditioning unit and noise disruptions. The resolution process includes:

- ✓ **Individualized Solution:** The hotel offers the guest a room upgrade to a quieter and more comfortable suite.
- ✓ **Apology:** The hotel manager personally meets with the guest to apologize for the inconvenience and assures them that their comfort is a top priority.

- ✓ **Service Recovery:** In addition to the upgrade, the hotel offers a complimentary spa treatment as a gesture of goodwill.
- ✓ **Feedback and Improvement:** The guest's feedback on the noise issues prompts the hotel to review and enhance its soundproofing measures for guest rooms, preventing similar complaints in the future.

By developing sound resolution strategies, offering appropriate remedies and compensation, and turning complaints into opportunities for service recovery, organizations can not only address immediate issues but also build stronger customer relationships and drive continuous improvement.

# Learning from Complaints

Complaints are more than just challenges to overcome; they are a rich source of feedback that can lead to continuous improvement. This chapter explores how to turn complaints into valuable feedback, implement changes based on insights from complaints, and effectively communicate these improvements to both customers and employees.

**Turning Complaints into Valuable Feedback for Continuous Improvement**

- ✓ **Feedback Collection:** Systematically collect and categorize feedback from complaints. This data can include common issues, recurring themes, and areas where your products or services fall short.
- ✓ **Root Cause Analysis:** Leverage root cause analysis to identify the fundamental reasons behind complaints. This reveals patterns and helps you address underlying issues.
- ✓ **Feedback Loops:** Establish feedback loops within your organization to ensure that complaints lead to action. Employees across all levels should be encouraged to contribute ideas based on feedback.
- ✓ **Data Analysis:** Use data analysis techniques to identify trends and patterns in the feedback. This can help you prioritize areas for improvement.

**Implementing Changes Based on Insights from Complaints**

- ✓ **Action Plans:** Develop detailed action plans for each issue identified through complaints.

These plans should include specific tasks, responsible individuals, and timelines.

- ✓ **Cross-Functional Teams:** Create cross-functional teams that collaborate to address issues. Involving individuals from different departments ensures a comprehensive approach to problem-solving.
- ✓ **Testing and Piloting:** Before implementing large-scale changes, test proposed solutions and pilot them in controlled environments to assess their effectiveness.
- ✓ **Continuous Monitoring:** After implementing changes, continuously monitor the impact. Use key performance indicators (KPIs) to measure progress and success.

**Communicating Improvements to Customers and Employees**

- ✓ **Transparency:** Be transparent about the changes you are making based on feedback. This builds trust and demonstrates your commitment to improving.
- ✓ **Customer Notifications:** For significant changes, proactively notify customers. Explain how these changes will benefit them and enhance their experience.
- ✓ **Feedback Acknowledgment:** Thank customers for their feedback and let them know how it contributed to positive changes. This encourages further feedback.
- ✓ **Employee Recognition:** Recognize and reward employees who have contributed to improvements resulting from feedback.

**Action Plan:**

- ✓ **Feedback Analysis Framework:** Develop a framework for analyzing feedback from complaints. This should guide your organization in systematically converting complaints into action items.

- ✓ **Change Management Protocol:** Establish a change management protocol that outlines how changes will be planned, implemented, monitored, and evaluated.
- ✓ **Feedback Recognition Program:** Create a program that recognizes employees who have played a pivotal role in identifying issues and contributing to improvements.

**Example:**

A software company receives several complaints about a recurring bug in their product. Through root cause analysis, they discover that the issue is related to a specific component. The company implements changes as follows:

- ✓ **Feedback Collection:** They document each complaint, categorize them, and analyze the nature of the bug and its impact on users.
- ✓ **Root Cause Analysis:** It's revealed that the bug is a result of conflicting code in a component of the software.
- ✓ **Action Plans:** They create a detailed plan to rewrite the code and thoroughly test it. A cross-functional team consisting of developers, testers, and product managers collaborates on this project.
- ✓ **Communication:** The company sends notifications to affected customers about the upcoming software update, which will resolve the bug. They acknowledge the complaints and explain how customer feedback drove the improvement.

- ✓ **Monitoring:** After the update, the company continuously monitors bug reports. They see a significant reduction in bug-related complaints, indicating the success of their changes.

This example illustrates how complaints, when turned into valuable feedback, can lead to targeted improvements, resulting in a better customer experience and a more robust product.

By systematically collecting feedback, implementing changes based on insights, and effectively communicating these improvements, organizations can not only address specific issues but also drive continuous improvement and demonstrate a commitment to customer satisfaction.

# Empowering Employees and Frontline Staff

Empowering employees, especially frontline staff, is pivotal to effective complaints management. This chapter delves into the significance of training employees to handle complaints professionally and efficiently, fostering a positive attitude toward complaints as opportunities for growth, and recognizing and rewarding outstanding complaints handling.

**Training Employees to Handle Complaints Professionally and Efficiently**

- ✓ **Complaint Handling Training:** Develop a comprehensive training program focused on complaint handling. This should cover active listening, empathy, resolution strategies, and communication skills.
- ✓ **Role-Playing Exercises:** Use role-playing exercises to simulate common complaint scenarios. These exercises provide employees with practical experience in handling complaints.
- ✓ **Case Studies:** Use real-life case studies from your organization or industry to illustrate effective complaint handling and the impact of mishandling complaints.
- ✓ **Continuous Education:** Complaint handling skills should be continuously reinforced through ongoing education and training.

**Encouraging a Positive Attitude Towards Complaints as Opportunities for Growth**

- ✓ **Cultural Shift:** Promote a cultural shift within the organization where complaints are viewed as valuable feedback and opportunities for growth rather than inconveniences.

- ✓ **Leadership Buy-In:** Leadership should set the tone by embracing complaints as sources of improvement and demonstrating the value of customer feedback.
- ✓ **Feedback Channels:** Create easy-to-use feedback channels for employees to report complaints or suggest improvements within the organization.
- ✓ **Rewarding Innovation:** Encourage employees to develop innovative solutions based on complaints. Recognize and reward those who contribute positively to the resolution of complaints.

**Recognizing and Rewarding Outstanding Complaints Handling**

- ✓ **Recognition Programs:** Establish a recognition program for employees who consistently handle complaints effectively and contribute to improvements.
- ✓ **Peer Recognition:** Encourage peer-to-peer recognition for outstanding complaint handling. This promotes a culture of teamwork and support.
- ✓ **Incentives:** Consider providing monetary or non-monetary incentives for exceptional complaint resolution and customer service.

**Action Plan:**

- ✓ **Complaint Handling Curriculum:** Develop a comprehensive curriculum for complaint handling training, including modules on active listening, empathy, resolution, and communication.

- ✓ **Complaint Handling Simulations:** Implement regular complaint handling simulations or role-playing sessions to keep employees' skills sharp.
- ✓ **Innovation Forums:** Create forums or platforms where employees can share innovative solutions developed based on complaints, fostering a culture of improvement.

**Example:**

A retail chain notices a dip in customer satisfaction scores related to in-store service. They implement an employee empowerment program:

- ✓ **Training:** They launch a training program for all frontline staff, focusing on complaint handling. This program includes active listening techniques, empathy-building exercises, and best practices in resolving common customer issues.
- ✓ **Role-Playing:** Monthly role-playing exercises are conducted in-store, allowing employees to practice complaint handling scenarios and receive feedback from supervisors.
- ✓ **Feedback Channels:** An internal feedback platform is introduced, where employees can report service issues they've identified in the store.
- ✓ **Recognition Program:** The company initiates a "Service Excellence Award" recognizing employees who consistently excel in handling customer complaints and contribute innovative ideas for improving service.

Over time, this program leads to a notable improvement in customer satisfaction scores and empowers employees to take a proactive role in service quality.

This chapter underscores the importance of empowering employees in complaints management. Proper training, fostering a positive attitude toward complaints, and recognizing outstanding performance all contribute to an organization's ability to transform complaints into opportunities for growth and improvement.

# Importance of Measuring and Evaluating Complaints Management

Effectively managing complaints is not just about resolution but also about continuous improvement. In this chapter, we delve into how to measure and evaluate your complaints management system. This includes identifying key performance indicators, utilizing data and analytics for improvement, and integrating complaints management with overall performance evaluation.

**Key Performance Indicators for Complaints Management Success**

- ✓ **Complaint Resolution Time:** Measure the average time it takes to resolve complaints. Shorter resolution times often indicate efficient complaint management.
- ✓ **Complaint Closure Rate:** Calculate the percentage of complaints that are successfully resolved and closed. A higher closure rate suggests effective management.
- ✓ **Customer Satisfaction:** Regularly survey customers who have filed complaints to assess their satisfaction with the resolution process and outcomes.
- ✓ **Repeat Complaints:** Track the number of customers who file multiple complaints. A decrease in repeat complaints indicates improved service.
- ✓ **Net Promoter Score (NPS):** Assess whether customers who've filed complaints would still recommend your organization to others.

- ✓ **Cost of Complaint Management:** Analyze the cost incurred in managing complaints, including staff time and resources.

**Using Data and Analytics to Identify Areas for Improvement**

- ✓ **Data Collection:** Use a comprehensive system to collect and store complaint data. This system should include information such as the nature of the complaint, resolution time, and outcomes.
- ✓ **Analysis:** Regularly analyze complaint data to identify recurring issues, trends, or patterns. This can involve statistical analysis and data mining techniques.
- ✓ **Root Cause Analysis:** Identify the root causes of complaints through data analysis. This enables you to address underlying issues.
- ✓ **Predictive Analytics:** Use predictive analytics to anticipate potential complaints based on historical data, allowing you to take proactive measures.

**Integrating Complaints Management with Overall Performance Evaluation**

- ✓ **Key Performance Indicators Alignment:** Ensure that the key performance indicators for complaints management align with broader organizational goals and key performance indicators.
- ✓ **Balanced Scorecard:** Implement a balanced scorecard approach that considers customer perspectives, internal processes, learning, and financial outcomes. Complaint management should be a part of this scorecard.

- ✓ **Employee Performance Metrics:** Include complaint management as a component of employee performance metrics and evaluations. This emphasizes the importance of effective complaint handling.

**Action Plan:**

- ✓ **Key Performance Indicator Development:** Define specific key performance indicators for complaints management in your organization.
- ✓ **Data and Analytics Infrastructure:** Establish or enhance data and analytics infrastructure to collect, store, and analyze complaint data effectively.
- ✓ **Integrating Complaints Management:** Align complaints management with overall organizational performance evaluation and ensure that this alignment is communicated to all relevant stakeholders.

**Example:**

A telecommunications company identifies customer complaints related to service outages as a recurring issue. They take several actions:

- ✓ **Key Performance Indicators:** They introduce key performance indicators, such as "Time to Restore Service," "Repeat Complaints After Outages," and "Customer Satisfaction Post-Outage Resolution."
- ✓ **Data and Analytics:** The company implements a robust data analytics system that not only records complaints but also monitors the network for potential issues. It uses predictive analytics to anticipate and address outages before customers notice.
- ✓ **Integrating with Performance Evaluation:** The complaint management KPIs become

integral to the company's balanced scorecard approach, ensuring that all departments, from technical teams to customer service, are evaluated based on their contributions to resolving customer complaints.

This comprehensive approach leads to a significant reduction in service outage-related complaints and higher customer satisfaction.

By identifying key performance indicators, utilizing data and analytics for improvement, and integrating complaints management with overall performance evaluation, organizations can continuously enhance their complaint management systems and, in turn, their overall performance and customer satisfaction.

# Key Steps in Measuring and Evaluating Complaints Management

Measuring and evaluating complaints management is crucial for organizations to assess the effectiveness of their complaint handling processes, identify areas for improvement, and make data-driven decisions to enhance customer satisfaction. Here's a detailed example of how an organization can measure and evaluate complaints management:

- ✓ Step 1: Establish Key Performance Indicators (KPIs)
  Strategy: Determine the KPIs that align with the organization's goals and reflect the effectiveness of complaint handling. Common KPIs include complaint resolution time, customer satisfaction scores, complaint recurrence rates, and employee feedback on complaint handling.
  Example: A retail chain identifies the following KPIs to measure complaints management effectiveness: average resolution time, customer satisfaction ratings, the percentage of complaints resolved within target timelines, and the number of repeat complaints for the same issue.
- ✓ Step 2: Data Collection and Management
  Strategy: Implement a robust system to collect, categorize, and manage complaint data consistently.
  Example: The retail chain adopts a comprehensive complaint management software that records all complaints, including details like the date of submission, category,

customer information, assigned handlers, and resolution outcomes.

- ✓ Step 3: Analyzing Complaint Data
  Strategy: Regularly analyze complaint data to identify trends, recurring issues, and areas for improvement.
  Example: The retail chain conducts monthly reviews of complaint data, analyzing patterns such as product-related issues, service quality concerns, and peak complaint periods.
- ✓ Step 4: Benchmarking and Comparison
  Strategy: Compare the organization's complaint handling metrics with industry benchmarks and best practices to assess performance.
  Example: The retail chain compares its average resolution time and customer satisfaction scores with industry standards and other leading retailers in the market.
- ✓ Step 5: Feedback Collection
  Strategy: Gather feedback from complainants about their satisfaction with the resolution process and the effectiveness of complaint handling.
  Example: The retail chain sends post-resolution surveys to customers, requesting feedback on their experience with the complaint resolution process.
- ✓ Step 6: Employee Feedback
  Strategy: Solicit feedback from employees involved in the complaint handling process to identify challenges and potential areas for improvement.
  Example: The retail chain conducts employee feedback sessions to gather insights from

customer service representatives, frontline staff, and managers on their experiences in handling complaints.

- ✓ Step 7: Root Cause Analysis

  Strategy: Perform root cause analysis for significant or recurring complaints to identify underlying issues.

  Example: The retail chain conducts a root cause analysis when they observe an increasing number of complaints related to product defects, leading them to identify a flaw in the supplier's manufacturing process.

- ✓ Step 8: Implementing Improvements

  Strategy: Based on the insights from data analysis and feedback, make necessary improvements to the complaint handling process.

  Example: The retail chain develops a training program for customer service representatives to enhance their complaint resolution skills and improve communication with customers.

- ✓ Step 9: Reviewing Progress

  Strategy: Regularly review progress against the established KPIs and assess the impact of implemented improvements.

  Example: The retail chain holds quarterly review meetings to assess whether the implemented training program has reduced complaint resolution time and improved customer satisfaction.

- ✓ Step 10: Continuous Monitoring

  Strategy: Continuously monitor complaint data and feedback to ensure ongoing improvement and maintain high standards of complaint management.

Example: The retail chain uses real-time dashboards to monitor complaint handling metrics and promptly address any emerging issues.

By following these steps, organizations can effectively measure and evaluate their complaints management process. The insights gained from this evaluation empower them to make data-driven decisions, enhance customer experiences, and build a reputation for excellent complaint resolution. Continuous monitoring and improvement ensure that the organization stays proactive in addressing customer concerns and fostering a customer-centric culture.

# Dealing with Difficult Situations

Handling escalated complaints, navigating legal and regulatory issues, and addressing widespread complaints or scandals require a high level of expertise and diplomacy. In this chapter, we explore how to manage these challenging situations effectively.

**Handling Escalated Complaints with Diplomacy and Tact**

- ✓ **Active Listening:** Begin by actively listening to the complainant's concerns. Show empathy and acknowledge their frustration.
- ✓ **De-escalation Techniques:** Use de-escalation techniques to calm an upset complainant. This can involve agreeing with their feelings or concerns without admitting fault.
- ✓ **Resolving the Issue:** If possible, attempt to resolve the issue promptly or explain the steps being taken to address it.
- ✓ **Offering Alternatives:** Provide alternative solutions or remedies if the initial complaint cannot be resolved as expected.
- ✓ **Escalation Protocol:** If the complaint remains unresolved, be transparent about the escalation protocol and the steps that will be taken next.

**Navigating Legal and Regulatory Implications of Certain Complaints**

- ✓ **Legal Compliance:** Ensure your complaint management process complies with relevant laws and regulations. Seek legal counsel to understand the implications of specific complaints.

- ✓ **Document Everything:** Maintain thorough records of the complaint, the steps taken to address it, and any legal advice received.
- ✓ **Communication:** Communicate with the complainant in a way that doesn't compromise your legal position. Admitting fault prematurely can have legal repercussions.
- ✓ **Cooperate with Authorities:** If regulatory bodies or authorities become involved, cooperate fully and transparently. Seek to resolve issues to avoid legal action if possible.

**Crisis Management: Addressing Widespread Complaints or Scandals**

- ✓ **Swift Response:** React promptly to widespread complaints or emerging scandals. Delays can lead to a loss of public trust.
- ✓ **Transparent Communication:** Communicate transparently with customers and the public. Explain the issue, the steps being taken to address it, and the measures in place to prevent it from happening again.
- ✓ **Media and PR Strategy:** Develop a media and public relations strategy to manage the narrative. Appoint a spokesperson or team to handle media inquiries.
- ✓ **Internal Investigation:** Conduct a thorough internal investigation to identify root causes and prevent recurrence.
- ✓ **Preventative Measures:** Implement immediate changes to prevent the issue from recurring, and communicate these changes to customers.

**Action Plan:**

- ✓ **Escalation Guidelines:** Develop a clear and documented escalation protocol for handling difficult complaints, ensuring that all employees are trained on its use.
- ✓ **Legal Consultation:** Establish relationships with legal counsel who specialize in the areas relevant to your industry. Seek their advice in advance to understand potential legal implications.
- ✓ **Crisis Management Team:** Assemble a crisis management team responsible for addressing widespread complaints or scandals. This team should include PR experts, legal counsel, and senior management.

**Example:**

A pharmaceutical company receives complaints about adverse reactions to one of their medications. Some of these cases are severe, and the issue becomes widely publicized. Here's how they address the situation:

- ✓ **Handling Escalated Complaints:** The company's customer service team is trained to actively listen to patients' concerns, express empathy, and offer immediate assistance. They provide alternative medications, financial support, and medical advice when necessary.
- ✓ **Navigating Legal and Regulatory Implications:** The company immediately contacts their legal counsel to understand the potential legal implications and regulatory actions. They cooperate fully with health authorities.
- ✓ **Crisis Management:** A crisis management team is formed, consisting of the company's CEO, legal counsel, public relations experts,

and regulatory affairs personnel. They engage with the media, provide transparent updates, and offer support to affected patients. Simultaneously, an internal investigation is conducted to understand the root cause and prevent future occurrences.

Through a coordinated and transparent approach, the company manages to regain public trust, ensure the medication's safety, and make significant changes to their quality control processes.

This chapter emphasized the importance of diplomacy and tact when dealing with escalated complaints, navigating legal and regulatory issues, and addressing widespread complaints or scandals. By following established protocols and crisis management strategies, organizations can successfully manage challenging situations and maintain their reputation and credibility.

# Key Challenges Organizations Face when having to Deal with Complaints

Emotional Nature of Complaints:

- ✓ Challenges: Dealing with emotional complaints can be challenging as it requires complaint handlers to navigate the complainant's strong feelings, such as frustration, anger, or disappointment. Emotional customers or employees may express their grievances passionately, making it essential to respond with empathy and understanding.
- ✓ Example: A customer files a complaint about receiving a damaged product after waiting for a long delivery time. The customer is upset and expresses their dissatisfaction through a series of emotionally charged messages. The organization's complaint handler must remain composed and respond with empathy, acknowledging the customer's frustration while reassuring them that the issue will be promptly resolved.

Resolving Complex Issues:

- ✓ Challenges: Some complaints involve multifaceted issues that require thorough investigation and collaboration across different departments. Resolving such complex complaints can be time-consuming and may require specialized expertise to identify and address the root causes adequately.
- ✓ Example: A customer files a complaint about recurring billing errors and poor customer

service. Investigating the complaint reveals that the billing system and customer database are not fully integrated, leading to frequent errors. Resolving this issue requires coordination between the IT, finance, and customer service departments to streamline processes and prevent future errors.

Escalated Complaints:

- ✓ Challenges: Certain complaints may escalate to higher levels within the organization, requiring the involvement of senior management or executives. Handling escalated complaints demands a delicate balance of providing a prompt resolution while ensuring the complainant feels heard and respected.
- ✓ Example: A dissatisfied customer escalates their complaint to the CEO after experiencing repeated issues with a product and inadequate support from the customer service team. The CEO must step in to address the complaint personally, ensuring the customer's concerns are addressed and providing a resolution that exceeds expectations.

Regulatory Compliance:

- ✓ Challenges: In some industries, complaints may involve legal or regulatory implications. Organizations must navigate compliance requirements carefully to avoid potential legal consequences and ensure that complaint handling practices adhere to industry standards.
- ✓ Example: A pharmaceutical company receives a complaint about adverse effects from a medication. Handling this complaint involves

adhering to strict reporting and documentation requirements set by regulatory authorities to ensure patient safety and comply with pharmaceutical industry regulations.

Communication and Response Time:

- ✓ Challenges: Providing timely and effective responses to complaints is essential. Organizations must have efficient communication channels and well-trained complaint handlers to address issues promptly. Delays in response or inadequate communication can exacerbate the situation and harm the organization's reputation.
- ✓ Example: A customer submits a complaint via email, expecting a response within 24 hours, as stated in the organization's customer service policy. However, due to a lack of streamlined communication processes, the complaint is not addressed until several days later, leading to further frustration for the customer.

Internal Complaints:

- ✓ Challenges: Organizations may face challenges when handling complaints from their employees. Addressing internal grievances while ensuring confidentiality and fairness can be complex, as it involves navigating HR policies and addressing potential conflicts within the organization.
- ✓ Example: An employee files a complaint about workplace harassment by a colleague. The HR department must conduct a thorough and confidential investigation, ensuring the complaint is addressed objectively while

safeguarding the well-being and rights of both the complainant and the accused employee.

Consistency in Complaint Handling:

- ✓ Challenges: Ensuring consistent complaint handling across various channels and departments is essential for building trust with customers. Lack of consistency in complaint resolution can lead to a disjointed customer experience and undermine efforts to resolve issues effectively.
- ✓ Example: A customer files a complaint via the company's website, seeking a refund for a defective product. The initial response from the customer service team acknowledges the complaint but fails to provide a clear timeline for resolution. Subsequently, when the customer follows up via phone, another representative provides a different response, leading to confusion and dissatisfaction.

Turning Complaints into Opportunities:

- ✓ Challenges: Viewing complaints as opportunities for improvement rather than mere problems can be challenging for some organizations. Transforming complaints into actionable insights for business growth requires a proactive and positive mindset towards feedback.
- ✓ Example: An organization receives multiple complaints about long wait times and a lack of information during the customer service phone support process. Instead of viewing these complaints as a burden, the organization's management uses the feedback to revamp their phone support system, reducing wait

times and providing automated updates to customers on their position in the queue.

Cultural Resistance:

- ✓ Challenges: Establishing a complaint-friendly culture may face resistance within some organizations. Overcoming resistance to change and promoting a culture that values feedback and continuous improvement requires leadership support and employee buy-in.
- ✓ Example: In a traditional organization, employees are hesitant to report internal issues or complaints, fearing retaliation or dismissal. Implementing a new open-door policy and encouraging transparent communication requires strong leadership commitment and a shift in the organizational culture to promote trust and openness.

Data Management and Analysis:

- ✓ Challenges: Collecting and analyzing complaint data can be overwhelming, particularly for organizations receiving a high volume of feedback. Implementing effective data management and analysis processes is crucial for gleaning actionable insights and identifying trends.
- ✓ Example: A large e-commerce platform receives thousands of customer complaints daily. Managing and analyzing this vast amount of data manually becomes impractical. To overcome this challenge, the organization invests in a robust complaint management system that automates data collection, categorization, and analysis, allowing them to

identify recurring issues and prioritize improvements efficiently.

Addressing these challenges requires a proactive and customer-centric approach to complaints management. By continuously improving complaint handling processes, investing in training and resources, and fostering a culture that values feedback, organizations can effectively turn complaints into opportunities for growth and build stronger relationships with their stakeholders.

# Steps and Strategies- Right from Receipt of Complaint to it Being Resolved and Afterwards

Step 1: Receiving the Complaint

- ✓ Strategy: Implement user-friendly and accessible complaint submission channels, such as email, phone, online forms, or in-person.
- ✓ Example: A retail company provides multiple channels for customers to submit complaints, including a dedicated customer service email, a toll-free helpline, and a feedback form on their website.

Step 2: Acknowledging the Complaint

- ✓ Strategy: Respond to the complainant promptly to acknowledge receipt of their complaint and set expectations for resolution timelines.
- ✓ Example: Upon receiving a complaint about a delayed delivery, an e-commerce company sends an automated email to the customer within 24 hours, assuring them that their complaint is being addressed and that they will receive a resolution within three business days.

Step 3: Active Listening and Empathy

- ✓ Strategy: Train complaint handlers to actively listen to the complainant's concerns, show empathy without admitting fault, and reassure the customer that their complaint is being taken seriously.

- ✓ Example: A hotel front desk staff member listens attentively to a guest's complaint about a noisy room, apologizes for the inconvenience caused, and assures the guest that they will investigate and find a suitable solution.

Step 4: Investigating the Complaint

- ✓ Strategy: Gather all relevant information and evidence related to the complaint to understand the root cause and identify any systemic issues.
- ✓ Example: An airline receives multiple complaints about baggage mishandling on a specific route. The customer service team collaborates with the baggage handling department and identifies a pattern of mishandling at a particular airport, leading to corrective actions and retraining of baggage handlers.

Step 5: Resolving the Complaint

- ✓ Strategy: Offer appropriate remedies or compensation based on the severity of the complaint and the impact on the complainant.
- ✓ Example: A restaurant receives a complaint from a customer about finding a foreign object in their meal. The restaurant manager immediately offers a sincere apology, refunds the meal cost, and provides a complimentary meal voucher for the customer's next visit as a gesture of goodwill.

Step 6: Communicating the Resolution

- ✓ Strategy: Ensure clear and timely communication with the complainant, keeping them informed about the resolution process and any necessary follow-up actions.

- ✓ Example: A software company resolves a technical issue reported by a customer and sends a personalized email, explaining the actions taken to address the problem, as well as steps to prevent a recurrence.

Step 7: Continuous Improvement

- ✓ Strategy: Use feedback from complaints to identify areas for improvement and implement necessary changes to prevent similar issues in the future.
- ✓ Example: A car manufacturer receives complaints about a recurring brake issue in a specific model. The engineering team conducts an in-depth analysis, identifies a design flaw, and recalls affected vehicles for free brake replacements, ensuring future models are improved.

Step 8: Follow-up and Feedback

- ✓ Strategy: After resolution, seek feedback from the complainant to gauge their satisfaction and learn about any remaining concerns.
- ✓ Example: A mobile service provider follows up with a customer whose complaint about network coverage was resolved. The customer expresses satisfaction with the solution and provides valuable feedback, enabling the provider to optimize their network services further.

Step 9: Record Keeping and Analysis

- ✓ Strategy: Maintain a comprehensive database of complaints, track trends, and analyze data to identify recurring issues and measure the organization's complaint resolution performance.

- ✓ Example: An online retailer uses complaint data to identify common reasons for returns, enabling them to collaborate with suppliers to improve product quality and reduce return rates.

Step 10: Employee Recognition and Training

- ✓ Strategy: Recognize and reward employees who excel in complaint resolution and provide ongoing training to equip employees with the necessary skills to handle complaints effectively.
- ✓ Example: A call center implements a "Star Performer" program, acknowledging complaint handlers who consistently receive positive feedback from customers. The program motivates employees to continue delivering exceptional service.

By following these steps and implementing the associated strategies, organizations can effectively handle complaints, improve customer satisfaction, and enhance their overall reputation. Properly resolving complaints not only leads to loyal customers but also provides valuable insights for continuous improvement and business growth.

# Fostering a Complaint-Friendly Culture

Fostering a complaint-friendly culture requires a comprehensive approach that involves both leadership commitment and employee engagement. Here are step-by-step procedures to establish a culture that values complaints and promotes proactive resolution:

Step 1: Leadership Commitment

- ✓ Strategy: Top-level management should prioritize complaint management and communicate its significance to the entire organization.
- ✓ Example: The CEO of a telecommunications company emphasizes the importance of complaints as opportunities for improvement during a company-wide town hall meeting, setting the tone for the organization's complaint-friendly culture.

Step 2: Transparent Communication

- ✓ Strategy: Promote open and transparent communication channels, encouraging employees and customers to voice their concerns without fear of reprisals.
- ✓ Example: An insurance company implements a confidential online complaint submission form accessible to all employees, ensuring anonymity for those raising internal concerns.

Step 3: Training and Education

- ✓ Strategy: Provide training to employees at all levels on active listening, empathy, and effective complaint resolution techniques.

- ✓ Example: A retail chain conducts regular workshops for customer service staff, focusing on empathetic communication and techniques for de-escalating emotional complaints.

Step 4: Establishing Clear Policies and Procedures

- ✓ Strategy: Develop well-defined complaint management policies and procedures that outline the steps for handling complaints, including timelines for resolution.
- ✓ Example: A software development company implements a standardized complaint handling process that includes acknowledging complaints within 24 hours and resolving them within 5 business days.

Step 5: Empowering Frontline Staff

- ✓ Strategy: Empower frontline staff to resolve complaints independently up to a certain level, reducing the need for unnecessary escalations.
- ✓ Example: A hotel empowers its front desk staff to address minor customer complaints, providing them with the authority to offer immediate remedies, such as complimentary upgrades or discounts.

Step 6: Encouraging Feedback

- ✓ Strategy: Actively seek feedback from customers and employees, encouraging them to provide suggestions and complaints for continuous improvement.
- ✓ Example: An airline uses in-flight surveys to collect feedback from passengers, inviting them to share any concerns or issues they experienced during their journey.

Step 7: Feedback Analysis and Action

- ✓ Strategy: Analyze complaint data to identify trends and patterns, using insights to address underlying issues and implement improvements.
- ✓ Example: A healthcare provider conducts regular reviews of patient complaints, identifying recurring issues, and adjusting processes to enhance patient experiences.

Step 8: Recognition and Rewards

- ✓ Strategy: Recognize and reward employees who demonstrate exceptional complaint resolution skills and contribute to a complaint-friendly culture.
- ✓ Example: An e-commerce company introduces an "Above and Beyond" award, recognizing employees who consistently receive positive feedback from customers for their complaint handling.

Step 9: Continuous Improvement

- ✓ Strategy: Continuously review and refine the complaint management process based on feedback and changing organizational needs.
- ✓ Example: An IT company holds monthly improvement meetings to discuss recent complaints, brainstorm solutions, and implement changes to prevent similar issues.

Step 10: Celebrating Success

- ✓ Strategy: Celebrate successful complaint resolutions and share stories of positive outcomes to inspire others in the organization.
- ✓ Example: An online retail company shares success stories of complaints turning into opportunities for service recovery and customer loyalty in internal newsletters and team meetings.

By following these steps and continuously reinforcing the importance of complaints as opportunities for growth and improvement, organizations can foster a complaint-friendly culture. This culture leads to enhanced customer satisfaction, increased employee engagement, and an overall positive impact on the organization's reputation and success.

# The Role of Leadership and Organizational Culture

A complaint-friendly culture, driven from the top-down, is essential for effective complaints management. In this chapter, we explore the significance of leadership's role in promoting transparency, accountability, and embedding complaints management into an organization's values and mission.

**The Importance of a Complaint-Friendly Culture from the Top-Down**

- ✓ **Cultural Alignment:** Ensure that the organization's culture aligns with a commitment to addressing complaints and using them as catalysts for improvement.
- ✓ **Leadership Example:** Leaders should set an example by actively engaging with complaints, supporting the resolution process, and demonstrating a willingness to learn from feedback.
- ✓ **Empowerment:** Encourage employees at all levels to actively participate in the complaints management process and contribute to solutions.
- ✓ **Feedback Channels:** Establish open and accessible feedback channels for employees to voice concerns and ideas.

**Leadership's Role in Promoting Transparency and Accountability**

- ✓ **Transparency:** Leaders must lead by example by being transparent in how they handle complaints, communicate actions taken, and admit to mistakes when necessary.

- ✓ **Accountability:** Hold leaders, managers, and employees accountable for their roles in the complaints management process.
- ✓ **Training and Resources:** Ensure that employees have access to the necessary training and resources for effective complaint resolution.
- ✓ **Ethical Leadership:** Emphasize the importance of ethical leadership and decision-making in complaint management.

**Embedding Complaints Management into the Organization's Values and Mission**

- ✓ **Mission Statements:** Integrate the commitment to effective complaints management into the organization's mission statement.
- ✓ **Values and Principles:** Define values and principles that emphasize the importance of listening to customer and employee concerns and using these concerns to drive improvement.
- ✓ **Performance Evaluation:** Include complaints management as a component of leadership and employee performance evaluations.
- ✓ **Communication:** Regularly communicate the organization's dedication to addressing complaints and seeking continual improvement.

**Action Plan:**

- ✓ **Leadership Training:** Implement leadership training programs that emphasize the role of leadership in fostering a complaint-friendly culture.
- ✓ **Cultural Assessment:** Conduct cultural assessments to understand how complaints

are perceived and managed within the organization.

- ✓ **Mission and Values Integration:** Update the organization's mission and values to explicitly include a commitment to effective complaints management.

**Example:**

A large tech company adopts a complaint-friendly culture:

- ✓ **Cultural Alignment:** The organization reiterates its commitment to addressing complaints and valuing employee and customer feedback in its internal and external communications.
- ✓ **Leadership Example:** The CEO actively participates in a "Complaints Resolution Day" where they engage with customers' complaints directly, showing a commitment to addressing feedback and implementing improvements.
- ✓ **Feedback Channels:** The company establishes an internal platform where employees can report concerns, and a committee, led by a senior executive, is responsible for addressing these concerns.
- ✓ **Training:** Leaders across all levels participate in a training program focused on handling complaints with empathy and resolving them effectively.

This approach results in a culture where complaints are seen as opportunities for growth and improvement. Employee engagement improves, and customers feel heard and valued, ultimately leading to better products and services.

By setting an example, promoting transparency and accountability, and embedding complaints management into the organization's values and mission, leaders can create an environment where complaints are seen as valuable tools for growth and improvement.

# Sample Complaint Handling Scripts and Templates

Below are some sample complaint handling scripts and templates for various stages of the complaint management process:

Note: *It is essential to customize these templates to suit your organization's specific needs, including inserting your company's details, complaint reference numbers, and appropriate resolutions. These sample templates provide a framework to start with and can be adjusted as necessary for different scenarios.*

**Complaint Acknowledgement Email Template:**

Subject: Acknowledgment of Your Complaint

*Dear* (Customer's Name)

*I hope this email finds you well. I am writing to acknowledge the receipt of your recent complaint regarding (briefly mention the issue). We sincerely apologize for any inconvenience this may have caused you.*

*We take your feedback seriously, and our team is already investigating the matter to identify the root cause and find a resolution promptly. We aim to provide you with an update within [specify the timeframe] with a comprehensive plan for addressing your concerns.*

*If you have any additional information or details you would like to share, please don't hesitate to reply to this email or call our dedicated complaint hotline at (phone number).*

*Thank you for bringing this matter to our attention, and we appreciate your understanding while we work towards resolving it.*

*Best regards,*
(Your Name) (Your Title) (Company Name) (Contact Information)

**Complaint Resolution Letter Template:**
[Your Name] [Your Title] [Company Name] [Company Address] [City, State, ZIP Code]
[Date]
[Customer's Name] [Customer's Address] [City, State, ZIP Code]
Dear [Customer's Name],
Re: Resolution of Your Complaint - [Complaint Reference Number]
*I hope this letter finds you well. We are writing to inform you that we have successfully resolved your recent complaint regarding [briefly mention the issue].*
*After careful investigation and analysis, we have identified the root cause of the problem and implemented necessary measures to ensure it does not recur. We apologize for any inconvenience this may have caused and thank you for bringing this matter to our attention.*
*As a gesture of goodwill, we would like to offer you [specify the compensation or resolution, if applicable, e.g., a partial refund, a replacement product, or a discount on your next purchase]. This is in appreciation of your patience and understanding throughout the resolution process.*
*We value your feedback and remain committed to providing excellent products and services to our customers.*
*Should you have any further questions or concerns, please do not hesitate to contact our dedicated*

*customer service team at [customer service phone number] or [customer service email address].*
*Thank you for giving us the opportunity to address your concerns, and we hope to continue serving you in the future.*
*Best regards,*
*(Your Name) (Your Title) (Company Name) (Contact Information)*

**Customer Satisfaction Survey Template:**
*Dear (Customer's Name),*
*We hope that the issue you reported has been satisfactorily resolved. We highly value your feedback and would appreciate it if you could take a few moments to complete this brief survey. Your responses will help us enhance our services and better meet your needs.*
*On a scale of 1 to 5 (with 1 being "Very Dissatisfied" and 5 being "Very Satisfied"), please rate the following:*

- ✓ *How satisfied are you with the resolution provided for your complaint?*
  *1 2 3 4 5*
- ✓ *How would you rate the responsiveness and communication from our customer service team during the complaint resolution process?*
  *1 2 3 4 5*
- ✓ *Do you feel that your concerns were adequately addressed?*
  *Yes / No*
- ✓ *Would you recommend our company to others based on your overall experience with the complaint resolution?*
  *Yes / No*

- ✓ *Do you have any additional comments or suggestions on how we can further improve our complaint handling process?*

*Thank you for your time and valuable feedback. If you have any other concerns, please don't hesitate to contact us.*

*Best regards,*
(Your Name) (Your Title) (Company Name) (Contact Information)

# Case Studies of Successful Complaints Management

Here are two examples of successful complaints management case studies in different industries:

**Case Study 1:** Retail Industry - "Turning Dissatisfied Customers into Brand Advocates"

- ✓ Company: XYZ Electronics (fictitious name)
- ✓ Scenario: XYZ Electronics, a leading electronics retailer, received multiple customer complaints about delays in product deliveries, poor customer service, and issues with product quality. The complaints were affecting the company's reputation and customer retention.

**Complaint Management Approach:**

- ✓ Acknowledgment and Empathy: Upon receiving each complaint, XYZ Electronics promptly acknowledged the customer's concerns, expressing empathy for the inconvenience caused.
- ✓ Root Cause Analysis: The company conducted a thorough analysis of the complaints to identify common patterns and root causes behind the recurring issues.
- ✓ Resolution and Service Recovery: XYZ Electronics implemented a dedicated complaint resolution team that prioritized resolving complaints promptly. The team provided appropriate remedies, such as expedited deliveries, discounts, and product replacements.

- ✓ Communication and Follow-up: Throughout the resolution process, the complaint resolution team communicated transparently with customers, providing updates on the status of their complaints and seeking feedback on the solutions provided.
- ✓ Continuous Improvement: XYZ Electronics used customer feedback from complaints to identify areas for improvement. They addressed operational inefficiencies, improved product quality, and enhanced customer service training for employees.

**Results:**

- ✓ Customer Satisfaction: The prompt and empathetic resolution of complaints led to increased customer satisfaction, with many customers expressing appreciation for the company's responsiveness and willingness to address their concerns.
- ✓ Customer Loyalty: By turning dissatisfied customers into satisfied ones, XYZ Electronics improved customer loyalty. Many customers who had experienced successful complaint resolutions became brand advocates, referring friends and family to the company.
- ✓ Reputation Enhancement: The company's commitment to resolving complaints and continuous improvement efforts led to a significant improvement in its reputation. Positive customer feedback and word-of-mouth referrals contributed to increased footfall and sales.

**Case Study 2:** Healthcare Industry - "Enhancing Patient Experience through Complaint Management"

Hospital: ABC Medical Center (fictitious name)
Scenario: ABC Medical Center, a renowned healthcare facility, faced several patient complaints related to long wait times, communication issues, and billing discrepancies. The complaints were affecting patient satisfaction scores and impacting the hospital's reputation.

**Complaint Management Approach:**

- ✓ Systematic Complaint Recording: ABC Medical Center established a centralized system for recording and tracking patient complaints. Each complaint was categorized based on the nature of the issue, enabling the hospital to identify common concerns.
- ✓ Timely Response and Investigation: The hospital ensured that every complaint received a timely response. A designated complaint handling team thoroughly investigated each case to understand the factors contributing to the complaints.
- ✓ Patient-Centered Solutions: ABC Medical Center emphasized patient-centered care in complaint resolution. Solutions were designed to address the specific needs and preferences of patients.
- ✓ Communication and Transparency: Throughout the resolution process, the hospital maintained open communication with patients, keeping them informed of progress and any necessary follow-up actions.
- ✓ Staff Training: ABC Medical Center provided comprehensive training to its staff on effective communication, patient handling, and customer service, aiming to prevent future complaints.

**Results:**

- ✓ Improved Patient Experience: The hospital's commitment to addressing complaints resulted in improved patient experiences. Patients appreciated the hospital's willingness to listen and take corrective actions.
- ✓ Higher Patient Satisfaction Scores: As complaints decreased, patient satisfaction scores rose significantly. Positive feedback from patients highlighted the positive impact of the hospital's complaint management efforts.
- ✓ Enhanced Reputation: The hospital's dedication to patient satisfaction and effective complaint handling contributed to an enhanced reputation in the healthcare community. Referrals from satisfied patients increased, bolstering the hospital's standing as a preferred healthcare provider.

Both of these case studies demonstrate the significance of effective complaints management in driving customer satisfaction, loyalty, and organizational reputation across different industries. Through a customer-centric approach and continuous improvement, organizations can successfully resolve complaints, turning dissatisfied customers into loyal advocates and positively impacting their bottom line.

# Interesting and Engaging Training Games to Enhance Understanding

Here are five training games on Complaints Management for managers to conduct with their teams. These games are designed to be engaging and interactive, enhancing participants' understanding of the subject. These training games can help reinforce the key concepts of complaint management while making the learning process engaging and fun, providing practical opportunities for employees to develop and apply their complaint resolution skills in a supportive training environment.

Each game includes its objectives, required materials, timing, how to conduct it, trainer observations, prompts for discussion, and the application of learning.

*(Examples of Role-play scenarios are in the next chapter. You can also develop your own examples)*

**Game 1: Complaint Resolution Role-Play**

Objective: Improve employees' complaint handling skills by simulating real-life scenarios.

Materials Required: Complaint scenarios, role-play guides, and evaluation forms.

Timing: 45 minutes to 1 hour.

How to Conduct:

- ✓ Prepare different complaint scenarios, varying in complexity.
- ✓ Assign participants to pairs or small groups, with one person playing the customer and the other playing the employee handling the complaint.

- ✓ Provide role-play guides outlining the complaint and the resolution process.
- ✓ Allow each pair or group to conduct the role-play.
- ✓ After each role-play, have the rest of the team provide feedback on what went well and what could be improved.
- ✓ Use evaluation forms to assess performance based on key criteria such as active listening, empathy, and resolution effectiveness.

Trainer Observations: Observe participants' communication skills, problem-solving abilities, and their demonstration of empathy during the role-play exercises.

Prompting Discussion: Discuss common challenges faced during complaint resolution and strategies for improvement. What techniques were most effective in resolving complaints during the role-play?

Application/Learning: Participants can apply the feedback and skills gained from the role-play exercises to real-life complaint resolution situations, improving their performance.

**Game 2: Complaint Category Sorting**

Objective: Enhance understanding of the different types of complaints and how to categorize them.

Materials Required: Complaint scenarios or cards, markers, and a whiteboard.

Timing: 30 minutes.

How to Conduct:

- ✓ Prepare a set of complaint scenarios or cards, each representing a different type of complaint (e.g., product quality, service, billing).
- ✓ Divide participants into teams.

- ✓ Provide each team with a marker and a set of complaint scenarios.
- ✓ In a limited time frame, teams must categorize and sort the complaints into appropriate categories on the whiteboard.
- ✓ Discuss the categorization and reasons behind the choices made by each team.

Trainer Observations: Observe how teams work together to categorize complaints and ensure they understand the different types of complaints.

Prompting Discussion: Discuss the importance of categorizing complaints accurately and how it helps in effective resolution.

Application/Learning: Participants will gain a better understanding of the common categories of complaints and how to categorize them for efficient handling.

**Game 3: Complaint Investigation Challenge**

Objective: Develop participants' problem-solving and investigation skills for handling complex complaints.

Materials Required: Complex complaint scenarios, pens, notepads, and a timer.

Timing: 45 minutes.

How to Conduct:

- ✓ Provide participants with a complex complaint scenario that includes multiple issues.
- ✓ Ask them to individually or in pairs investigate the complaint, identify the root causes, and develop a resolution plan within a time limit.
- ✓ After the time is up, participants present their findings and resolution plans.
- ✓ Encourage discussion and feedback on the effectiveness of the investigation and the proposed resolutions.

Trainer Observations: Observe participants' analytical skills, investigation methods, and creativity in developing resolution plans.
Prompting Discussion: Discuss the challenges of handling complex complaints and the importance of thorough investigation.
Application/Learning: Participants can apply the problem-solving and investigation techniques learned to real-world complaints that require in-depth analysis.

**Game 4: Complaint Resolution Challenge**
Objective: Enhance participants' skills in resolving complaints under time pressure.
Materials Required: Timer, fictional complaints, and resolution criteria.
Timing: 30 minutes.
How to Conduct:

- ✓ Provide participants with fictional complaints and a set amount of time to resolve each one.
- ✓ Use a timer to keep participants on track.
- ✓ The complaints should vary in complexity and require different approaches to resolution.
- ✓ After each round, discuss the effectiveness of the resolutions and the challenges faced.

Trainer Observations: Observe how participants handle time pressure, make decisions, and prioritize resolution steps.
Prompting Discussion: Discuss the impact of time pressure on complaint resolution and strategies for efficient handling.
Application/Learning: Participants can improve their ability to handle complaints quickly and make effective decisions under time constraints.

**Game 5: Complaint Metrics Quiz**

Objective: Reinforce understanding of key complaint management metrics.

Materials Required: Quiz questions, answer sheets, and pens.

Timing: 20 minutes.

How to Conduct:

- ✓ Create a quiz with questions related to complaint management metrics (e.g., First Contact Resolution rate, Net Promoter Score, Customer Satisfaction Score).
- ✓ Participants answer the questions individually or in teams.
- ✓ Review the answers and discuss the importance of each metric in complaint management.

Trainer Observations: Assess participants' knowledge of complaint management metrics.

Prompting Discussion: Discuss how tracking and analyzing complaint management metrics can lead to process improvements.

Application/Learning: Participants can apply their knowledge of key metrics to measure and evaluate the effectiveness of complaint management in their roles.

# Complaint Scenarios, Role-play Guides, and Evaluation Forms for use in the Training/ Games/Sessions

Here are five complaint scenarios, role-play guides, and evaluation forms for use in training sessions on complaint management:

**Complaint Scenario 1: Product Quality Issue**
Scenario: A customer purchased a smart-phone from your electronics store, but it developed a significant technical issue within a week.
Role-Play Guide:
Participant 1: The Customer (complaining about the defective smart-phone).
Participant 2: The Employee (responsible for handling the complaint).

Evaluation Form:
Active Listening (1-5):
- ✓ 1: Minimal active listening.
- ✓ 5: Exceptional active listening skills.

Empathy (1-5):
- ✓ 1: Lacks empathy.
- ✓ 5: Demonstrates deep empathy with the customer's frustration.

Resolution Effectiveness (1-5):
- ✓ 1: Unable to provide a satisfactory resolution.
- ✓ 5: Provides a satisfactory resolution to the customer's issue.

**Complaint Scenario 2: Billing Discrepancy**

Scenario: A long-time customer has noticed discrepancies in their monthly billing statements, with unauthorized charges.

Role-Play Guide:

Participant 1: The Customer (complaining about billing issues).

Participant 2: The Employee (responsible for handling the complaint).

Evaluation Form:

Active Listening (1-5):

- ✓ 1: Minimal active listening.
- ✓ 5: Exceptional active listening skills.

Empathy (1-5):

- ✓ 1: Lacks empathy.
- ✓ 5: Demonstrates deep empathy with the customer's concerns.

Resolution Effectiveness (1-5):

- ✓ 1: Unable to provide a satisfactory resolution.
- ✓ 5: Provides a satisfactory resolution and addresses the billing discrepancies.

**Complaint Scenario 3: Service Quality Complaint**

Scenario: A hotel guest is dissatisfied with the quality of service they received during their stay.

Role-Play Guide:

Participant 1: The Hotel Guest (complaining about service quality).

Participant 2: The Hotel Staff (responsible for handling the complaint).

Evaluation Form:

Active Listening (1-5):

- ✓ 1: Minimal active listening.
- ✓ 5: Exceptional active listening skills.

Empathy (1-5):

- ✓ 1: Lacks empathy.
- ✓ 5: Demonstrates deep empathy with the guest's concerns.

Resolution Effectiveness (1-5):

- ✓ 1: Unable to provide a satisfactory resolution.
- ✓ 5: Provides a satisfactory resolution, addressing the service quality concerns.

**Complaint Scenario 4: Delivery Delay**

Scenario: An e-commerce customer is upset because their order, which was supposed to arrive in two days, has been delayed by a week.

Role-Play Guide:

Participant 1: The Customer (complaining about the delivery delay).

Participant 2: The Customer Service Representative (responsible for handling the complaint).

Evaluation Form:

Active Listening (1-5):

- ✓ 1: Minimal active listening.
- ✓ 5: Exceptional active listening skills.

Empathy (1-5):

- ✓ 1: Lacks empathy.
- ✓ 5: Demonstrates deep empathy with the customer's frustration.

Resolution Effectiveness (1-5):

- ✓ 1: Unable to provide a satisfactory resolution.
- ✓ 5: Provides a satisfactory resolution, addressing the delivery delay.

**Complaint Scenario 5: Inadequate Product Support**

Scenario: A software customer is dissatisfied with the lack of technical support provided after purchasing a software product.

Role-Play Guide:

Participant 1: The Customer (complaining about inadequate product support).

Participant 2: The Technical Support Representative (responsible for handling the complaint).

Evaluation Form:

Active Listening (1-5):

- ✓ 1: Minimal active listening.
- ✓ 5: Exceptional active listening skills.

Empathy (1-5):

- ✓ 1: Lacks empathy.
- ✓ 5: Demonstrates deep empathy with the customer's concerns.

Resolution Effectiveness (1-5):

- ✓ 1: Unable to provide a satisfactory resolution.
- ✓ 5: Provides a satisfactory resolution and addresses the inadequate product support concerns.

These complaint scenarios, role-play guides, and evaluation forms are designed to help employees practice their complaint resolution skills in a controlled setting. They can be customized to suit the specific needs and challenges of your organization.

# Taking it Forward

In this final chapter, we will summarize the key takeaways from the book, reinforce the value of effective complaints management, and encourage readers to implement the strategies and techniques discussed.

**Summarizing Key Takeaways**

- ✓ **Complaints as Opportunities:** Complaints are not nuisances but opportunities for growth and improvement. By listening to customers and employees, organizations can uncover valuable insights.
- ✓ **A Complaint-Friendly Culture:** Fostering a culture that embraces complaints from the top-down is essential. Leaders should actively engage with complaints and demonstrate the importance of feedback.
- ✓ **Complaint Management Process:** Establishing a clear, step-by-step complaints management process ensures that complaints are handled efficiently and effectively.
- ✓ **Empathy and Resolution:** Active listening and empathy play a pivotal role in complaint resolution. Employees should be trained to handle complaints with care and professionalism.
- ✓ **Data and Analytics:** Using data and analytics to measure and evaluate complaints management allows organizations to identify areas for improvement.
- ✓ **Leadership and Culture Integration:** Leadership's commitment to transparency, accountability, and embedding complaints

management in the organization's values is crucial.

**Reinforcing the Value of Effective Complaints Management**

Effective complaints management fosters trust and loyalty in several ways:

- ✓ **Improved Reputation:** Swift and empathetic handling of complaints enhances an organization's reputation. Customers and employees perceive the organization as one that cares about their concerns.
- ✓ **Customer Loyalty:** Satisfied customers are more likely to remain loyal and recommend the organization to others. By resolving complaints effectively, an organization can retain its customer base.
- ✓ **Employee Morale:** An organization that actively listens to employee concerns and values their feedback fosters a positive work environment. This, in turn, leads to higher employee morale and retention.
- ✓ **Continuous Improvement:** Effective complaints management leads to continuous improvement in products, services, and internal processes.

**Encouraging Readers to Implement Strategies**

To put the knowledge gained from this book into action, readers are encouraged to:

- ✓ **Audit Current Practices:** Conduct an audit of the organization's current complaints management practices to identify areas that need improvement.
- ✓ **Establish Clear Protocols:** Develop clear protocols for complaint submission, handling,

and resolution. Ensure these are communicated across the organization.

- ✓ **Training and Development:** Invest in employee training to enhance their complaint handling skills. This includes active listening, empathy, and resolution strategies.
- ✓ **Data-Driven Decision Making:** Use data and analytics to monitor complaint trends, identify recurring issues, and make informed decisions for improvement.
- ✓ **Leadership Involvement:** Engage leadership in the complaints management process. Ensure they actively participate in resolving escalated complaints and demonstrate the value of feedback.
- ✓ **Cultural Shift:** Foster a cultural shift that views complaints as opportunities for growth and improvement. This shift should encompass both employees and customers.

**Action Plan:**

- ✓ **Organizational Assessment:** Conduct an assessment of the organization's current culture and complaints management practices.
- ✓ **Implementation Roadmap:** Develop a roadmap for implementing the strategies discussed in this book, including timelines and responsible individuals or teams.

**Example:**

A medium-sized e-commerce company reads this book and decides to implement the knowledge gained:

- ✓ **Organizational Assessment:** The company conducts a thorough assessment of its current complaints management process. They identify several areas for improvement, including the need for more comprehensive training for customer service representatives.

- ✓ **Implementation Roadmap:** They create an implementation roadmap, which includes hiring a professional trainer for customer service staff, revamping their complaint handling procedures to include clearer escalation processes, and launching a customer feedback campaign to encourage complaint submissions.

By actively implementing these strategies, the company improves its complaint handling, leading to a rise in customer satisfaction and loyalty.

In closing, this chapter reinforces the vital role of effective complaints management in building trust, loyalty, and improvement. It encourages readers to take the knowledge gained from this book and put it into practice by assessing their current practices, establishing clear protocols, investing in training, using data-driven decision-making, involving leadership, and fostering a complaint-friendly culture. Through these actions, organizations can transform complaints into valuable opportunities for growth and positive change.

# Conclusion

In the realm of Complaints Management, we have explored the intricacies of turning customer feedback into a powerful tool for growth and excellence. Throughout this journey, we have discovered that complaints are not mere irritations but invaluable sources of insight, guiding organizations towards continuous improvement.

We have witnessed the significance of understanding the psychology behind complaints, recognizing that emotions and experiences drive the voice of both customers and employees. By implementing active listening and empathy, organizations can bridge the gap between dissatisfaction and resolution, nurturing long-lasting relationships with their stakeholders.

The art of categorizing complaints has allowed us to discern patterns and trends, distinguishing individual incidents from systemic issues. Armed with this knowledge, businesses can devise targeted solutions and address root causes, effectively eliminating recurring complaints.

Through a step-by-step guide to building an effective complaints management process, we have emphasized the importance of establishing clear timelines, user-friendly complaint channels, and assigning responsibilities. Moreover, by involving relevant stakeholders and adopting a proactive approach, organizations can swiftly respond to complaints and avert potential crises.

Investigating complaints with integrity has shown us the path to fair resolution, even in the face of difficult situations. By navigating legal and regulatory implications and crisis management scenarios with diplomacy and transparency, organizations can protect their reputation and build trust with their customers.

At the core of this journey lies leadership and organizational culture. We have reinforced the impact of a complaint-friendly culture that values feedback and seeks opportunities for growth. When complaints management is seamlessly woven into an organization's values and mission, it becomes a driving force for continuous improvement and success.

As we reach the end of this book, we encourage you to embark on your own complaints management odyssey. Armed with the tools, strategies, and insights provided here, you have the power to transform complaints into stepping stones towards excellence.

We hope that the knowledge gained from these pages will empower you to build stronger relationships with your customers, strengthen your brand reputation, and position your organization as a leader in customer satisfaction. By embracing complaints management, you will discover the remarkable potential for growth and innovation hidden within customer feedback.

Thank you for accompanying us on this journey of Complaints Management.

May you step confidently into a future where every complaint is an opportunity for progress and success.

## About the Author 'GERARD ASSEY'

Gerard Assey is a Graduate in Economics, a PGD in Management (HRD) and holds a Doctorate in Leadership. Gerard holds several International Qualifications in Sales, Debt Collection, Training & Teaching, and is a 'Fellow' of the prestigious 'Institute of Sales & Marketing Management'-UK, a Certified NLP Practitioner, a 'Certified Trainer', an 'Accredited Management Teacher-Behavioral Sciences', a 'Certified Competency Facilitator', a 'Certified Management Consultant'- (the International credentials of a professional management consultant, awarded in accordance with global standards of the ICMCI); and a Certification from the University of Michigan in 'Successful Negotiation: Essential Strategies and Skills'

He is also a Member of the 'National Association of Sales Professionals' backed with several years experience in varied industries, both in India and Overseas. He also holds an 'Etiquette Consultant' Certification from the USA (by Sue Fox, Author of Best Seller: 'Business Etiquette for Dummies'. She has trained some of the top celebrities' world over). He was also a recipient of a scholarship for extensive training in Japan on 'Corporate Management for India'.

Gerard Assey is 'Founder & Chief Corporate Trainer' of the Group: '**Citius, Altius, Fortius Unlimited'**- an organization that **celebrated 20 years of Glorious Service** in 2021, focusing on 3 Core Competencies:

**People. Performance. Profit**; in functional areas of Sales & Marketing, HR & Organizational Development, covering Recruitment, Training & Consultancy!

Having managed organizations with large Sales Forces in India & Overseas, his specialization cover extensive areas of Sales Training (All levels - Presentation, Negotiation, Key/ Strategic Accounts Management & Managerial Skills for all sectors), Bid Proposal/ Capture Planning/ Management Trainings, Retail Sales, Customer Service & Customer Retention Programs, Training for Prevention & Collection of Debt, Self & Personal Development Programs (Time Management, Teamwork & Team Building, Business Etiquette & Personal Grooming, Leadership & Managerial Skills, People Management Skills, Train-the-Trainer etc), including preparation of Custom-designed Business Manuals for Internal (HR, Induction, and Sales etc) & External use (Instruction, User Manuals).

Gerard has successfully conducted over 6000 Trainings & Workshops (as of Oct '23) all across India, Middle East, Africa, Europe & S.E. Asia. Besides public programs conducted regularly, both in India & Overseas, he has some of the top names as clients whom he services from Single Owners to large Public & Government undertakings, covering all sectors, for their in-house needs.

His website: www.CollectionSkills.com is the only one in this part of the world to be featured in the 'Collections & Credit Risk Magazine-USA' under 'Who's Who in Training' and ranks TOP, along with other websites listed below on most search engines.

Gerard is author of 86 books already (Oct 2023),

A few of the business related books being:

1. Bite-sized Bits on Commonsense Management
2. Heart to Heart on Life's Principles'
3. How to become a Successful Manager
4. The Sales Professionals' Master Workbook of S.Y.S.T.E.M.S
5. The Professional Business Email Etiquette Handbook & Guide
6. The Professional Business Video-Conferencing Etiquette Handbook & Guide
7. Professional Presentation Skills
8. Exceptional Customer Service
9. Professional Tele-Marketing Skills
10. Professional Debt Collection Skills
11. The G.R.E.A.T. Sales & Service Workbook
12. Sales Training Advantage for Results (*The Ultimate Sales Training Manual to enable you stand out as a S.T.A.R.*)
13. CEO Daily Planner & Organizer
14. The Sales Professionals' Master Daily Planner
15. The Professional Debt Collector's Master Daily Planner
16. My Daily Planner & Organizer
17. MY EMERGENCY INFORMATION RECORD (Family Emergency & Peace of Mind Planner)
18. The Ultimate Therapist & Counselors Planner and Organizer
19. Building an Ethical Workplace
20. Managing Relationships at Work
21. Managing Business Meetings Effectively
22. Effective Delegation Skills
23. Goal Setting for Success
24. B2B Selling by Email
25. Professional Business Etiquette & Grooming
26. Dining Etiquette & Table Manners
27. Effective Networking Skills
28. Grooming, Etiquette & Manners for Teens, Young Adults & Future Leaders
29. Inter-Personal Skills
30. Get Ready, Get Hired!
31. Selling in a Recession

32. Effective Receivables Management in an Economic Downturn!
33. Real Estate & Property Sales Training
34. Credit Sales & Accounts Receivable Management
35. Selling Skills for Real Estate & Property Advisors
36. Take G.R.E.A.T. C.A.R.E!
37. Spa, Salon & Health Club Selling Skills
38. Selling Travel, Holiday & MICE Services
39. Selling Skills for Spa's, Salons & Health Clubs
40. Retailing in Salons & Spas
41. Selling Holiday, Vacation, Tours & Packages
42. The Power of Sales Referrals
43. Selling Luxury
44. Technical Selling Skills
45. Financial Advisors Sales Training
46. Dealing with Burnout at Work Monopolize Your Markets
47. Selling to Affluent Customers
48. Growing up with Grace
49. Financial Selling Skills
50. *The Effective Manager's Guide: Key Skills to Thrive*
51. From Aspiring to Inspiring: A Guide for New Managers on the Rise
52. The Power of Focus
53. Selling with Integrity: Sell Like Jesus The Perfect Role Model!
54. 31 Habits of Champions: Your 31-Day Journey to Greatness
55. Rejecting Grasshopper Talk: From Grasshopper to Giant-Killer-*Defeating Giants Daily!*
56. Navigate the AI-Powered Future of Bid & Proposals: Up-Skill to Stay Relevant with Alternative Career Paths & Opportunities
57. Hiring Sales Winners
58. Present with Impact
59. Success Unlocked: *Breaking Free from Habits that Hold You Back*
60. Complaints to Cheers, Feedback to Gold: Mastering Complaints Management

Besides regularly contributing to business & trade journals, including international ones such as the 'Creative Training Techniques' and the 'Sales News' of the U.S.A, He is also a member of several prestigious bodies & trade associations, having participated in many Conferences & Workshops in India & Overseas.

Prior to his last assignment of leading & managing a large MNC as head, Gerard had a 3-year stint in the Middle East as a Consultant with a leading British Consultancy Firm.

As the past 'Official Country Representative' for the International Business Award- 'THE STEVIES'-(the business world's own Oscar) for about 4 years- he ensured a few Indian companies that qualify for the same every year!

Gerard can be contacted at:
Email: training@Sales-Training.in,training@CollectionSkills.com
Websites:

www.Sales-Training.in
www.EtiquetteWorks.in
www.CollectionSkills.com
www.RetailSalesTraining.in
www.SalesTrainingIndia.com
www.ManualPreparation.com
www.TrainingWithPuppets.com
www.FirstContactAcademy.com
www.SalesAndMarketingRecruiter.com

## Our TRAININGS & BOOKS that can help your team

- ✓ **Sales Effectiveness**: Selling Skills for any Sector: Service/ Logistics/ FMCG Realty/ Insurance & Finance/ Media/ SPA's, Health Clubs & Salons/ Key Account Management, Effective Negotiation Skills/ Bid & Proposal Management Skills/ Retail Sales Training: Any Sector (Auto, Jewelry, Clothing, Luxury etc)
- ✓ **Customer Service Skills**-Complaints Handling & Customer Retention
- ✓ **Debt Prevention & Collection Skills**
- ✓ **Etiquette & Grooming**
- ✓ **Leadership & Managerial Skills**
- ✓ **Self & Personal Development Skills**: Presentation Skills/ Effective Communication Skills/Business Proposal Writing Skills/ Problem Solving & Decision Making Skills/ Empowering Secretaries-The perfect PA! (For Secretaries & PA's)/ Effective Time Management/ Teamwork & Teambuilding/ P.R.I.D.E- **P**ersonal **R**esponsibility **I**n **D**elivering **E**xcellence

www.ingramcontent.com/pod-product-compliance
Lightning Source LLC
Chambersburg PA
CBHW062110160726
48282CB00026B/742
* 9 7 8 9 3 9 2 4 9 2 8 0 8 *